100 IDEAS FOR ENJOYING THE GREAT GAME OF GOLF

The
GOLF
BUCKET LIST

JEFF THORESON

To golf and all the opportunities it has provided
and doors it has opened for me.

• • • • • • •

an imprint of Ulysses Press
PO Box 3440
Berkeley, CA 94703
www.velopress.com

VeloPress is the leading publisher of books on sports for passionate and dedicated
athletes around the world. Focused on cycling, triathlon, running, swimming,
nutrition/diet, and more, VeloPress books help you achieve your goals and reach
the top of your game.

ISBN: 978-1-64604-685-0
Library of Congress Control Number: 2024931672

Printed in the United States
10 9 8 7 6 5 4 3 2 1

Project editor: Bridget Thoreson
Managing editor: Claire Chun
Copy editor: Renee Rutledge
Proofreader: Joyce Wu
Front cover design: Raquel Castro
Interior design: what!design @ whatweb.com
Artwork from shutterstock.com: numbered list icon © Vector-Icon; pages 6, 25, 178
    © Agor2012; pages 13, 29, 51, 71 © Zapatosoldador; page 109 © Lucky Creative

Contents

Special Features

Introduction

Hello. I am a human being. In all my decades of writing, I have never felt the need to qualify myself as such because the species of anyone whose name appears as the author of anything has always been obvious. But now, after more than 40 years of tapping out stories, columns, essays, and books—starting in the waning days of the manual typewriter to now, as I sit at the ultra-sleek keyboard of my spanking new MacBook—I need to assure you that I am a living, breathing mass of flesh and that the experiences that follow were undertaken by this mass of flesh. No AI was used in creating this book.

These experiences and observations are accumulated over 40 years of playing this disobliging game and a quarter of a century of traveling around the world in pursuit of new experiences, with golf as the catalyst. I feel quite fortunate to have been able to undertake these experiences and, quite frankly, I have not yet gotten to a few of them. For some of these bucket list experiences, I relied on friends who have done them or occasionally just good old-fashioned reporting, which is how I got my start as a writer. But most of the suggestions in this book stem from my personal experiences and observations of playing this game with friends, family, fellow competitors, and the occasional stranger.

Golf, narcotic pastime that it is, has taken me to many far-reaching extremes of this planet, and for that I am grateful. It has fostered enduring friendships with people I otherwise would have never met and without whom my life would be less rich because without them, some of these experiences never would have happened. Should any of those friends read this book, they may recognize themselves in these stories.

As you read, I suspect my affection for links golf will become quite apparent. If you haven't played the great seaside courses of the British Isles, perhaps some of my writings will inspire you to do so. They are among the most attainable bucket list experiences as well as the experiences that I have found to be most unforgettable. In my decades of travel, I have lost track of the number of times I have set off on such journeys, but I have not lost track of the courses I've played—the great ones, the hidden gems, and the ordinary—or the friends I have played them with. And to you, my reader, I offer these personal stories and experiences—things artificial intelligence couldn't possibly relate—and I challenge you to undertake some, or many. Your golfing journey, your life journey, will be enhanced by it.

As a writer, I hate AI and I have a growing distain for humans who think I can be replaced by a soulless digital technology. As a consumer, I am quite aware of artificially created books that may draw readers with pretty covers but contain little substance beyond the regurgitation of facts and glaring lack of emotion. On these pages I have avoided dictating what your golf bucket list should look like. I have no monopoly on golf wisdom. I can't tell you how many golf courses there are in Ireland, or Scotland, or England, or Wales. But I can relate the experience of playing the game in those destinations. So rather than telling you what courses your bucket list should include (there are plenty such bucket list musings on the internet), I urge to you crave the experiences golf offers outside of your home course and contemplate the game not as shots and rounds and scorecards collected but as an extension of your being, human as it is.

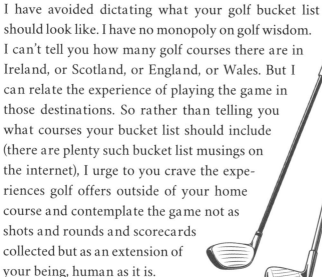

CHAPTER 1

10 Tee Shots You Need to Hit

NO. 1 THE OLD COURSE AT ST. ANDREWS

You can stand on the first tee at Pebble Beach Golf Links and wonder what all the fuss is about. You can belly up, pay your green fee, and get your ass kicked on the first tee at the Bethpage Black Course or Pinehurst No. 2 or Tournament Players Club (TPC) Sawgrass. You can stride snobbishly off the first tee at Augusta National Golf Club, Cypress Point Club, or Pine Valley Golf Club and in relative secrecy, just as you can off the first tee at many of the world's great courses— except one. The first tee of the Old Course at St. Andrews is different.

This is the game's most-hallowed ground. You may have plotted and planned, scrimped and saved for years. You may have dared to dream of playing this course. But when you get to the first tee of the Old Course at St. Andrews, you will have to hit your first tee shot in front of what might seem like half of the "Auld Grey Toon," Scottish brogue for this small town of drab stone buildings and often overcast skies. There is no lack of well-stocked, comfortably stooled imbibing establishments here, but townsfolk and visitors prefer to mill about the first tee and watch nervous golfers from around the world try not to embarrass themselves with questionable swings and sometimes shameful results.

Here, you'll notice tradesmen, craftsmen, and shop owners lollygag past on their lunch hour or on their way to or from work on those lusciously long Scottish summer days when you can tee off at six in the evening and still get in 18. Tourists, some golfers and some not, will gather along the white rail fence that separates the first tee and adjacent eighteenth green from the town, as if watching a long shot head down the backstretch. Guests at the hotel across the street from the eighteenth fairway will peer out their hotel room windows, and St. Andrews members will watch you from the clubhouse window.

Caddies and players with upcoming tee times and players who aren't even playing until tomorrow, or later in the week or whenever the St. Andrews Links Trust lottery dictates, will be soaking up the atmosphere at the oldest course in the world—the course where the game started long before Christopher Columbus set sail for a new world.

When you are here in the middle of it all, you will be taunted by the ghosts of Bobby Jones, Harry Vardon, and Old and Young Tom Morris, knowing that every great player who has ever played the game has stood on the exact plot of grass you nervously occupy. Here, shepherds and shopkeepers have been whacking balls or stones around since about the time Joan of Arc was burned at the stake. Turns out she was a martyr, wrongly accused, and eventually beatified and canonized. But you will feel like the world is closing in on you standing there in front of everyone with your driver, hoping to get your golf ball airborne and land it somewhere in the town greensward that doubles as the widest fairway in the world. And then, before you do anything wrong or anything right, the starter will bark: "The 10:10 group, play away please." And everyone will turn to watch the 10:10 group. Your group.

This place is different, old and stone gray, a town that could easily have fallen to ruin had it not been for golf. If you compared an image of the first and eighteenth holes from the early days of photography to the one you will take with your smartphone a few hours after you tee off as you cross the Swilken Bridge, the course, the clubhouse, and the town backdrop will all look remarkably the same in both the grainy black-and-white and the new digital image.

To the sheepherders who swatted stones with sticks into rabbit holes on this land, their blood-to-Scotch ratio likely well past the legal limit, you with the 10:10 starting time owe a debt of gratitude, as do I. To Archbishop Hamilton, whose 1552 proclamation seeded the town's linksland to the people for golf, "if that's how they intend to use it," you owe a debt of gratitude, as do I.

I've been in the 10:10 group. I've been in the 3:10 group and a couple of other groups. I know the sudden churning of the gut that comes with the starter's command. You'll look around, and it'll be as if you're in one of those movie sequences where the camera is panning and the people, the town, and the whole world close in around you. Every other first tee shot in the world is cake compared to the first at St. Andrews—a shot to a fairway wider than a soccer pitch, which, without the history, without the surroundings, without the pressure, without peering eyes of everyone in town, would be one of the easiest shots in the wide world of golf.

I've heard the murmurs after hitting a good shot. "Ahhh, at's fein shoot laddie." And I've heard the cackles after squibbing it. "Didn't quite get all of that one, did you, mate?"

Either way, you'll be off to plot your way around the most sacred turf in sports. And four hours later, not a minute longer, your caddie will see to it that you will have a chance to redeem yourself in front of a new gathering that lines the white fence rail and quite possibly some blue-blazered, crested-tied members in the clubhouse washing down haggis with a 25-year-old single malt and watching your approach shot to the last green from clubhouse window. Play well.

NOTES

. . . .

. . . .

. . . .

. . . .

❏ **NO. 1 THE OLD COURSE AT ST. ANDREWS** Date:. . . . .

NO. 1 MACHRIHANISH GOLF CLUB

"All of Scotland is to the right," your caddie will tell you, "Don't miss left." On the first tee at Machrihanish Golf Club near Campbeltown, Scotland, you will stand somewhat confused, somewhat dumbfounded, somewhat angry. Who in the world would build a course that requires you to lace the ball across the frothing Atlantic Ocean (if the tide is in; across the beach if it's out) to land on a narrow strip of fairway that also heaves like the ocean—all on your first swing?

I agree with those who argue that this is the hardest opening tee shot in the world. While St. Andrews has the history, inquisitive onlookers, and pressure of following in the footsteps of the sport's greatest players, the first at Machrihanish has relative anonymity; and it has meanness. It is a hard-as-nails tee shot, unlike almost any other in the world. The opening tee shot at Machrihanish offers equal parts trepidation and exhilaration. It's as thrilling as it is difficult. It's the greatest bite-off-as-much-as-you-can-chew tee shot in the world. At a brutal 430 yards long, the hole doglegs to the left and hangs on the ocean's edge for the duration. If you rinse your first shot of the day, it will wear on you as you play one of the great courses of Scotland. Any little right-to-left movement of this first tee shot likely means your ball will spend eternity in a cold saltwater bath.

This shot was the vision of Old Tom Morris way back in 1879. He, of course, is the famous St. Andrews clubmaker turned golf professional whose record as a player had no equal in his time. He made his way to Machrihanish at a time when traveling across the body of Scotland then down the "Long and Winding Road" (Paul McCartney wrote that famous Beatles song just a few miles from Machrihanish at his High Park Farm) on the "Mull of Kintyre" (another McCartney song, this time with his band Wings) was even more difficult than the harrowing five-hour drive along narrow, winding roads that you'd take today. Maybe Old Tom was just pissed off. So, he designed the toughest tee shot on the course, maybe the toughest tee shot in Scottish golf or perhaps the whole world of golf, and requires you to hit it on your first shot of the day.

I've come all that way to face this shot I've heard so much about. It was early morning and a mist was rolling in from the sea (just as McCartney described). I hit the shot well. But it was hard to see, you know, with the mist and all. Did it fly far enough? Did I bite off more than I could chew? I don't know. But I was satisfied. I'd given it my best, and if that wasn't good enough for Old Tom and Machrihanish, so be it. Hopefully yours will be.

NOTES

. . . .

. . . .

. . . .

. . . .

❏ **NO. 1 MACHRIHANISH GOLF CLUB** Date: . . . .

NO. 17 TOURNAMENT PLAYERS CLUB AT SAWGRASS

Golf—pleasingly or exasperatingly—is just golf. Other sports teach equality and teamwork and that great things can be accomplished if everyone does their best, works together, and lifts each other up for the common good. Golf will have none of that. Golf teaches that the world is a cruel, harsh place; that the cosmos couldn't care the hell less that you broke 80 last week. With every new round, you must prove yourself again.

The game doesn't care about what anyone else can do for you but only what you can do for yourself. It cares not about how much money you make, your IQ, or your lineage but only that you rise to the occasion because in golf and in life a man makes his own breaks, pulls his own weight, carries his own bag. Faced with adversity, a man stares it down, looks it squarely in the eye, and accepts the challenge. In golf, a man doesn't look around for help, for someone to hand off to, for someone to relieve him of the need to accept responsibility for his actions. There is a whole world of influence working on every moment of your life, but the total control that golf offers to manage your own destiny is scarce in life. And nowhere is it more tested than at the seventeenth hole of the Stadium Course at the Tournament Players Club (TPC) at Sawgrass.

This hole—the most famous par 3 in golf and perhaps the most famous hole, period—doesn't care who you are—president or plebeian, king or commoner. It doesn't care whether you're a CEO, Tiger Woods, a day laborer from Yonkers, or you or me. It cares only that you pick the right club, make an exacting strike, and properly account for the day's elements. In the seventeenth at Sawgrass we find the very reason we are drawn to the game—because golf, unlike most other aspects of our lives—gives you the wheel to steer and no one is going to jump in the driver's seat and bail you out. Life's other endeavors all have some sort of an opposing force conspiring against us, the yin of a nice paycheck against the yang of career drudgery.

In ancient Chinese thought, yin and yang are not opposites, not good vs. evil. They are all the complementary forces of the world without which the world would not exist.

But on the seventeenth at TPC Sawgrass there is only yin. You. Against the most famous shot in golf. And when you get there, you'll have parted with many of your pretty pennies, but you'll be in complete control. The hole is just as happy to issue you a quadruple bogey with two balls in the water that surrounds the island green or a birdie as the reward for a steely nerved tee shot. It's up to you.

Maybe you catch the seventeenth on a calm day, the water flat and reflective. Or maybe she's a little testy, like the grade-school teacher frayed to her last nerve. Or maybe she's just an outright bitch. But golf is not about fairness, so when it's your turn, accept your fate as being of your own doing. Tee it up, account for the elements, and hold the wheel tight.

On my day, the seventeenth played 135 yards to a back pin with a wind strongly from the right and slightly hurting. It's a little 9-iron, and I hit it good. Real good. Maybe great. But a gust of wind hits it, moves it left, and carries it on. My well-crafted shot lands near the back left of the green, bounces once, and disappears. It might have stayed up. It might have bounced over the bulkhead and rinsed. I march on to find out, to see if my best was good enough. It turns out my ball trickled onto the footpath that gets players to the green. I got it up and down for par. I considered my good fortune. Others have not been so lucky.

Does anyone claim equity in golf? In life? We swallow the bitter with the sweet and forge on to deal with the next injustice of golf—to yet again try to prove our mettle—just like everyone else who has come through the seventeenth hole on the Stadium Course at TPC Sawgrass. Your fate rests with only you.

NOTES

....
....
....
....

❏ **PINEHURST AND THE NORTH CAROLINA SANDHILLS**

Date: ....

NO. 17 THE OLD COURSE AT ST. ANDREWS

The seventeenth on the Old Course at St. Andrews—known as the "Road Hole"—contains three perilous elements: 1) the notorious pot bunker tucked connivingly into the left side of the green, 2) the road—yeah, an actual road—that picks the hole up at the tee box and meanders innocently enough down the right side of the fairway until it cuts left and juts just a few feet behind the green, 3) the tee shot, which is required to be played over a hotel—a real, modern, luxury hotel with guests and everything. It is quite possible and, in fact, very likely that a tee shot or two end up colliding with some portion of the hotel or its outbuildings every day. Phil Mickelson once curved his tee shot smack into the hotel and his ball came to rest on the patio of a ground-floor room.

As the course itself has been around for centuries and the hotel for just a few decades, one must wonder who had the audacity to build a hotel in the kink of a dogleg right fairway. Turns out, a railway station and its supporting buildings have occupied that spot since 1852, so while the hotel made the shot more interesting, it didn't really change the complexion of the shot. As the hole has been lengthened to accommodate the increasing distance players have been hitting the ball, the tee has been pushed back to require the tee shot to carry more of the hotel property.

When you step up to the seventeenth tee, you'll be confronted by a big dark-green Fenway Park–like wall with large letters spelling out OLD COURSE HOTEL in white. The old railway sheds are visible, but it's the yellow brick of the hotel with its abundance of plate-glass windows that draws your attention. Hit an old black railway shed— who cares? Taking out a glass window might have a more weighty consequence. Truth is, most of us everyday players have to hit the shot to the left, barely challenging the hotel grounds. It's the top players who come to St. Andrews every few years to compete in the Open Championship who must pick a letter on that wall to sail their ball over, hoping it clears the hotel grounds to a safe spot on the other side of the hotel grounds. Still, we everyday players are far more likely to squib one to the right or flat-out hit the shot in the wrong direction and send our golf ball rattling among awnings, gardens, or patios where guests might be sipping a happy hour cocktail.

It's a shot unlike any other in the world. I've taken my tries at it and always heeded the caddie's advice that safe is better than broken glass. But safe leaves you an unmanageable distance from the green, so I chip away at that distance, plotting to avoid the Road Hole bunker. Maybe your effort will be more exciting.

NOTES

. . . .

. . . .

. . . .

. . . .

❏ **NO. 17 THE OLD COURSE AT ST. ANDREWS** Date:. . . . .

NO. 7 PEBBLE BEACH GOLF LINKS

We laugh at short par 3s, the ones so diminutive even we average players need only a mashie (in the old days) or a wedge (today) to cover the negligible distance. We puff out our chests as we approach the tee, as if to say this shot is mere child's play. Often it is. But there are a few holes in the world where that brief distance requires more skill than most of us can muster. Such is the case at the Pebble Beach Golf Links seventh hole. This hole was once thought to be such a skimpy aspect of the course that the designer, William Herbert Fowler, said "the golfing shot required is not of such a character" as required by a championship course. "I think it would be quite easy to find another location for a one-shot hole to take its place," Fowler wrote in 1920, just a year after the course opened.

Thankfully, his partner, Jack Neville, recognized this as foolishness and retorted: "The seventh is a little gem of a mashie shot, only 106 yards and a drop of 40 feet from tee to green. The latter is surrounded on three sides by the bay. There is usually a little wind blowing on this point, which gives it every natural hazard to the golfer, making this hole one of the most interesting on the links." Now, more than a century later, this appetizing bite of golf along Carmel Bay on the Monterey Peninsula in California is not just one of the most interesting holes on the Pebble Beach links but one of the most interesting holes in the wide world of golf.

So, I stepped up to the seventh tee at Pebble Beach with a fair amount of wind blowing in from the ocean, and that mashie shot of yesteryear and the wedge shot of today has morphed into a full 7-iron, a club I would typically use to hit about 160 yards. Other players of much better caliber than I over the years have hit more club. It is famously told that iconic Bel-Air Country Club professional Eddie

Merrins once aced the hole in a ferocious wind that required him to hit a 3-iron. Legend also has it that fabled professional Sam Snead was once so unwilling to face the wind at No. 7 that he putted the ball off the tee and down the hill, and made par.

I didn't feel the putter would work, so I pulled the 7-iron. The wind pushed the ball to the right, and it looked like it was going over the cliff to the ocean. But somehow it dropped quickly and landed in the rough between the bunkers that cling to the edge of land. I hit my next shot a few feet from the hole and made the putt for par. Should Fowler and Neville have found another spot for a par 3 at Pebble Beach? The entire golfing world thinks not.

NOTES

. . . .

. . . .

. . . .

. . . .

❏ **NO. 7 PEBBLE BEACH GOLF LINKS** Date: . . . .

NO. 1 IN A REAL TOURNAMENT

Very few golfers—even good golfers—ever play in a real tournament. I'm not talking about a tournament you would see on television, the likes of which a very small percentage of golfers ever achieve the level of competence to take part in. But I'm also not talking about your club's member-guest tournament, or even the club championship.

These are cozy competitions where, yes, there is something on the line, but you're playing on a course you know with people you know. By "real tournament," I mean real golfers putting their game on the line against other real players in competition, where if you make a double bogey half the field couldn't care less and the other half wishes you made triple bogey.

When you play in a real tournament, you're nervous the night before. You pick at your dinner wondering if your game is up to the test of competing against players better than you. Your sleep is antsy. On the practice tee before the round, you're excited, and you look for ways to try to calm yourself. In a real tournament, they announce your name on the first tee then your gut rumbles because you have to put the tee in the ground, and in front of strangers, you have to try not to embarrass yourself. You have to hit a shot that counts. And then, you have to play all 18 holes, during which one of your fellow competitors will record every single stroke you take.

In a real tournament, no one gives you a 3-foot putt, and if your ball rolls into a divot, tough. It doesn't matter if you make a 2 or a 12, you hit the ball until it rolls off the face of the earth into the hole, and then you deal with the result. When you put your game on the line, in real competition, you learn about your game; you learn about yourself. You may not like what the lesson teaches, but you'll be better for it.

NOTES

....

....

....

....

❏ **NO. 1 IN A REAL TOURNAMENT** Date: ....

NO. 8 ROYAL TROON GOLF CLUB

In the modern game of golf, we equate length with difficulty. This is one of the sad aspects of what the game has become. Because professional golfers we see on television can reach 600-plus-yard par 5s with two voracious shots, length is now a critical component of our game. But in golf, short is not necessarily sweet. And, to this point, we find the eighth hole at the wonderful Scottish course of Royal Troon Golf Club one of the must-play courses for golfers visiting Scotland.

It is refreshing to see everything required to meet the test of greatness condensed into the aptly named "Postage Stamp" hole, of a distance so mere that almost everyone can cover it with a simple swing of a lofted club. If size does matter, then at the Postage Stamp hole it matters to the opposite—not because it is so big but because it lacks bigness. These days, it is not unusual for greens to be 10,000 square feet. The green at the Postage Stamp hole is but 2,636 square feet, and the fact that five bunkers—including one of particularly tight confines ominously named Coffin—guard its edges makes this quite possibly the most difficult 120-yard shot in the world.

When the world's best players come to Troon every decade or so to play the Open Championship, the Postage Stamp always delivers—both delight and disaster. And over a century of championships at Troon, the stories of both are legendary. The great Gene Sarazen, playing in his first Open Championship in 1923, made a double-bogey five on the hole and lost by a shot. In his last Open Championship in 1973 at the age of 71, he hit 5-iron into the wind and aced it. Fans love the hole because it can provide the sublime and the ridiculous. Birdies seem routine but are interspersed with players like Tiger Woods once taking six strokes to complete the par 3, or obscure German professional Hermann Tissies once taking 15.

Writing about the hole in *Golf Illustrated* in the 1880s, two-time Open champion Willie Park, Jr., described it as "a pitching surface skimmed down to the size of a postage stamp." In a game where golf holes are routinely lengthened to keep up with the pace of the modern game, this hole was shortened to add to the drama and intrigue. And you will find both when you get there.

NOTES

. . . .

. . . .

. . . .

. . . .

❏ **NO. 8 ROYAL TROON GOLF CLUB** Date: . . . .

NO. 1 THE OLD COURSE AT BALLYBUNION

If it weren't for its fabulous golf course, the small town of Ballybunion, Ireland, would be exactly what it has been for a millennium—a small seaside Irish town where nothing of significance ever happens beyond the occasional tourist bus rambling through so foreigners could take note of the ruins of the Ballybunion Castle, soak in the walk along the Bromore Cliffs, or more likely, lunch and imbibe in a town where pubs outnumber churches by quite a wide margin.

But there is a golf course. And about 50 years ago, golfers from around the world started coming here to play it, and they realized it was one of the world's finest—a links layout that shucks and jives through towering dunes, where quirkiness and challenge meet to create a thrill ride for you and your 14 clubs (and the many, many golf balls you will lose). So, rather than Ballybunion remaining a sleepy Irish town, its golf course attracts visitors by the bus load. They come only to play golf and then move on to the next Irish golfing town.

But these busloads of golfers who come and go have never seen anything quite like the tee shot on the first hole at Ballybunion Golf Club. The teeing ground sits right outside the clubhouse, and down the fairway to the right, the Killehenny Cemetery sits like a catcher's mitt waiting for your foul ball to plop down into it. If you think hitting a snap hook off the first tee at your home club is bad luck, what happens if you drop your first tee shot on one of the most famous courses in the world onto someone's final resting place?

I've hit this tee shot many times, always erring in favor of the two fairway bunkers to the left, preferring my ball to find its resting place there rather than disturbing the spirits of millennia gone by. The cemetery is so old, there is no real record of when the first soul was laid to rest there. The town's website dates it to "early Christian times," and for me, that's all the more reason to avoid it.

Early grave markers are weathered away, but burials continue to take place in Killehenny Cemetery. If your tee time coincides with such a ceremony, you'll be asked to play the forward tee, which takes the cemetery out of play. You'll graciously abide because that forward tee also takes the two fairway bunkers out of play. In many rounds across the Old Course at Ballybunion, I've never hit my first tee shot into Killehenny Cemetery. Friends have, often to be plagued with hauntingly bad rounds from there on. Make your best swing— to the left.

NOTES

. . . .

. . . .

. . . .

. . . .

❏ **NO. 1 THE OLD COURSE AT BALLYBUNION** Date: . . . .

NOS. 5–8 AND 15–17 CASA DE CAMPO'S TEETH OF THE DOG

Golf is relegated to your memories of last season's glory and your hopes for the season to come. Winter sucks, but the winter golf trip does not. For a couple of years a group of guys from my club chose the Dominican Republic as our getaway. Four days and three nights of wall-to-wall golf and evenings of alfresco dining in shorts and flip-flops. Late afternoons of snorkeling, then reclining on a lounge chair on the white-sand beach with a piña colada while I rotisseried my tan back from winter whiteness.

While the wind drifts snow halfway up the flagsticks of our home course, we play the famous Teeth of the Dog course with its spectacular string of pearl golf holes along the see-through Caribbean Sea. The first four holes serve the almost-sole purpose of getting your game from the clubhouse to the ocean. When you arrive amid the jaw-dropping scenery of swaying palm trees and impossibly blue water, you find the par-3 fifth hole, from which it would take little effort to jump off the tee box and splash down in the bathwater-warm

Caribbean. It's tempting, but your focus must turn to the moment's task, which is the daunting chore of ignoring the postcard scenery and hitting an 8-iron or so across a nibble of the Caribbean to a green that sits aside a jetty of rocks protecting it from the currents and tides that the sea throws its way.

Failure lies in the beauty of luscious aqua blueness. If you fail on this tee shot, when you get to the green, you will see the sad remains of your failed effort among hundreds of others resting on the coral beneath a few feet of water. But no worries, the Teeth of the Dog course offers you six more attempts to avoid the ocean.

While golf and the ocean meet in spectacular fashion all around the world, there are no such meetings where so many holes hang so tantalizingly close to the ocean, where the weather is so compatible with the game, where the water is so blue, and where the entire setting is so meditative—almost therapeutic—for the soul escaping the harshness of the golf-less winter back home.

NOTES

. . . .

. . . .

. . . .

. . . .

❏ **NOS. 5–8 AND 15–17 CASA DE CAMPO'S TEETH OF THE DOG** Date:. . . . .

NO. 5 LAHINCH GOLF CLUB

After the first time I played the oddity that is the Klondyke Hole, the short par-5 fourth at Lahinch Golf Club in Ireland, I wasn't sure what to think. A towering dune in the middle of the fairway blocks progress to the green, much like a linebacker blocks the way to the end zone on fourth and goal from the one-yard line.

Then, on the tee of the par-3 fifth, I stood confused. There was no green in sight. My caddie came to the rescue, leaned in, and explained the Dell Hole to me. The green was nestled among a cluster of 20-foot-high dunes, directly behind the dune 100 yards or so in front of me. He pointed down my sight line to a small white rock at the top of that dune and said that was the target line for today's pin. It was 145 yards. He handed me the 7-iron because the wind (there is always wind in Ireland) was coming from the left and hurting. He told me to accommodate by playing 10 feet left of the rock—as if I could've been that accurate with a shot that almost amounts to swinging with your eyes closed. No portion of the pin and no portion of the green was visible from the tee. And as a last piece of advice, he told me the green is plenty wide but very shallow, so distance was more important than direction.

I hit the 7-iron exactly where he asked, but it was drawing to the left, and the wind was eating it up. The genius of the design of this hole is that it plays into the prevailing wind off the Liscannor Bay of the North Atlantic, so you're supposed to play the shot up into the winds so it descends softly between the dunes. My ball was not descending softly. It plummeted behind the dune. The result was left to be defined until we got to the other side— as is the result of every shot no matter how well struck from the tee of the Dell Hole. But my caddie had seen this particular shot hundreds of times. "That's going to be a tough one," he reported.

All these years later, after many rounds across this wonderfully quirky links, Lahinch is my favorite course in the Republic of Ireland. It's so cool. No hole like the Dell will ever be built again, and while there are a few somewhat-similar holes around the world, the one-two punch of the Klondyke and the Dell is an experience unlike any other in golf.

NOTES

. . . .
. . . .
. . . .
. . . .

❏ **NO. 5 LAHINCH GOLF CLUB** Date:. . . . .

10 US Destinations You Should Experience

PINEHURST AND THE NORTH CAROLINA SANDHILLS

Had the wee Scottish golf pro Donald Ross not emigrated to the United States and taken up residence in the Sandhills of North Carolina, perhaps the area would still be the barren wasteland it was at the turn of the twentieth century. You could certainly make an argument that without Donald Ross's imprint, the region around Pinehurst may still have golf, but not the golf it has. Ross was a talented player brought to Pinehurst by the town's founder, James Tufts, a decision that changed golf not only in Pinehurst but throughout America.

During the 1880s, Tufts, tired of brutal New England winters, used the profits of a successful soda fountain business to head to the warmth of southern places like Florida or the Bahamas. Concerned that working-class New Englanders didn't have the resources for such a trip, he looked for a place where he could re-create everything rich and charming about New England, minus the winter cold. He was a regular on the north-south train route, getting off at various destinations, until one day in 1895 he disembarked in Southern Pines. He met brothers Henry and J. R. Page, and they cut a deal for 4,703 acres of sandy loam, thick with towering pines but thin on promise. Tufts had just sold his share in the American Soda Fountain Company for $700,000, a pittance of which he used to pay the Pages' asking price of $1.25 per acre, although some locals said he was swindled, claiming the land was worth only 85 cents an acre.

Tufts, not a robust man physically but quite robust in business, probably didn't care about the price per acre. He heard the Sandhills had a natural healing quality and was determined to build a town where New Englanders, many of whom suffered from tuberculosis and other ailments, could come to get healthy.

The oddity of the topography of south-central North Carolina—beach-like sand sprouting towering longleaf pine trees—would be otherwise insignificant if it weren't for the fact that the terrain, like the linksland of the British Isles, is so ideally suited for golf, which was no more in Tufts's original plan than a 16-story hotel. But Tufts's love of the wholesome, small-town virtues of New England transplanted into the more hospitable climate of North Carolina would evolve to become one of the world's great golf destinations.

He commissioned Ross to build four courses at his new resort in Pinehurst, and the young pro found his calling. Today, those four courses, including US Open venue Pinehurst No. 2, remain the centerpiece of golf at the resort that has grown to 10 courses while his work at nearby Pine Needles Lodge and Golf Club, Mid Pines Inn and Golf Club, and Southern Pines Golf Club create the attraction golfers gravitate to, complete with the charm of New England and the hospitality of the South. Thankfully, Ross ventured out from the Sandhills to design courses around the country, including all-time greats like Seminole Golf Club in Florida, Oakland Hills Country Club near Detroit, Oak Hill Country Club in Rochester, New York, Aronimink Golf Club near Philadelphia, Scioto Country Club in Columbus, Ohio, and East Lake Golf Club in Atlanta. In all, Ross designed about 400 courses around the county.

Since his death in 1948, dozens more modern courses have been built to supplement Ross's Pinehurst classics. Places like Talamore Golf Resort, Mid South Club, Tobacco Road Golf Club, and Legacy Golf Links have all become great complements to the main features. And it all started inadvertently when Tufts lured Ross to what was once considered a sandy, god forsaken wasteland.

. . . .

. . . .

. . . .

. . . .

❏ **PINEHURST AND THE NORTH CAROLINA SANDHILLS** Date: . . . .

THE SOUTH CAROLINA COAST

If Myrtle Beach is a smorgasbord of cheap seafood restaurants and gentlemen's clubs, perhaps it's only because the South Carolina coast needs a balance to the abundance of classy establishments of Charleston and Hilton Head Island. I'm not knocking Myrtle Beach, I'm just saying it's different. Clearly, its formula for drawing groups of golfers year-round has worked for decades. It is time-tested and proven, and without Myrtle Beach, American golf would lose a major appendage. But the entire coast of the Palmetto State is an attractive destination to the golfing population of the Northeast, Canada, and beyond.

Along the Grand Strand, which includes the entire Myrtle Beach area and even spills into southern North Carolina, there are more than 80 courses, although that number is down from more than 100 at Myrtle Beach's peak at the beginning of the century. Those left in the culled herd are largely the ones proven to be the best over the decades, from the historic Pine Lakes Country Club, which opened in 1927 as the first course in the beach resort area, to the wonderful

Dunes Golf and Beach Club designed by Robert Trent Jones in 1949, to modern gems like the four courses at Barefoot Resort and Golf and the Mike Strantz–designed Caledonia Golf and Fish Club. The Grand Strand's deep bench, improving food scene, and always prevalent nightlife keeps it among the world's greatest golf destinations.

The southern extreme of the Grand Strand almost melts into the northern reaches of Charleston, and if there is a classier city, I haven't been there. Charleston teems with history, museums, fine dining, beaches, and a downtown area with something interesting on every corner. Even the golf seems to be more stylish than in most cities. That's largely thanks to three islands:

- Kiawah Island is famous for its Ocean Course, which hosted the famous "War by the Shore" Ryder Cup in 1991, and its four supporting layouts are outstanding as well.

- Seabrook Island is more subdued and home to the Robert Trent Jones–designed Crooked Oaks and the more modern Ocean Winds, both of which roam through marsh, maritime forests, and centuries-old moss-hung oaks.

- On the Isle of Palms, the Links Course at Wild Dunes Resort rolls through dunes to the climatic oceanside finish. The Harbor Course isn't quite as wild but a fun routing nonetheless.

The mainland is anchored with courses like Dunes West Golf Club, RiverTowne Country Club, and the Links at Stono Ferry. And if there's any way you can possibly finagle a starting time at the private Yeamans Hall Club, you won't be disappointed by the reinvigorated Seth Raynor design from the 1920s.

Everything is considerably more modern on Hilton Head Island. It was 1969 when Jack Nicklaus helped a former insurance salesman from Indiana clear golf holes through the maritime forests of the island to create Harbour Town Golf Links at the Sea Pines Resort. It became a classic almost from the time the first tee shot was hit. The

Professional Golfers' Association of America (PGA) Tour event now known as the RBC Heritage has been played on the course since its opening. Much of the rest of the land on the island, which is a little more than half the size of Nantucket, is crammed with 29 courses and there's not a slouch among them.

NOTES

. . . .

. . . .

. . . .

. . . .

❏ **THE SOUTH CAROLINA COAST** Date: . . . .

THE MONTEREY PENINSULA

Hindsight being what it is, I now realize it was a mistake for me and three friends to fly across the country two days after New Year's Day for a tee time at Pebble Beach. The post-holiday crowds at the airport and the burden on the airlines to get everyone home caused lengthy delays I should have anticipated. Of course, it was my own fool self that booked a flight into San Francisco when San Jose is the appropriate and closer airport to the Monterey Peninsula. It all added up to a late-night landing, rental car fiasco, and drive into the small hours of the morning to a cheap hotel in Carmel-by-the-Sea.

I can't remember the name of the hotel, but there was some sort of tree involved, and approaching 2 a.m., it was finally in sight when the lights on the sign flickered out. By the time we'd negotiated the last traffic light and pulled up to the lobby door, it was dark inside and locked up tight. Unsure what to do, we drove a full lap around 17 Mile Drive, pulled into the parking lot at Pebble Beach, and tried to get some sleep.

I'm quite sure it's not among Fodor's travel tips to spend the night before your tee time at one of the world's most famous courses, hoping sleep will come in the bucket seat of a rental car. Fortunately, the rest of the trip went well. We got Pebble Beach on a glorious blue-sky day, and I made par on all of its seaside holes except at No. 8, where I made an "X." Spyglass Hill was the surprise of the trip.

A course just up 17 Mile Drive from Pebble and Cypress Point is no afterthought, and the Links at Spanish Bay is a surprisingly delightful nature links along the Pacific.

It will be among the most expensive bucket list trips you make, but these days that's the norm with bucket lists.

NOTES

· ·

· ·

· ·

· ·

❏ **THE MONTEREY PENINSULA** Date:· ·

BANDON DUNES GOLF RESORT

We East Coasters who are all privy to at least one major international airport can fly to the British Isles as quickly as we can get to the Bandon Dunes Golf Resort. So the question was always, "Why trade authentic links golf for an American impersonation?" But when you get to Bandon Dunes, you'll realize this isn't an impersonation of the linksland courses where the game began. It's true, pure, American links golf. It's a different ocean and a different style, but it's not hard to argue that it's every bit as good. If the soul of the game belongs to Scotland, the definition of what it inspires is found along this stretch of the Oregon coast.

The massive resort includes six courses that, like the great British Isles links, live in harmony with the land. Catch the sixteenth of the Bandon Dunes course on a clear late afternoon as the sun sets over the Pacific, and you'll know why you travel to play the game. The Sheep Ranch course has nine oceanside greens. Pacific Dunes may be the most natural of the courses, with fairways that roll and greens that fit perfectly among the sometimes-massive dunes. The Old Macdonald course, a tribute to the great classic-era designer Charles Blair Macdonald, celebrates classic design concepts and pays tribute to the traditions of the game. Bandon Trails works its way from atop a massive dune into maritime forests and back into the dunes. Bandon Preserve is a 13-hole par-3 course.

Other courses call themselves links courses, but they are the impersonators, mere attempts to copy what the game looks and feels like in its ancestral home. They always fall short. But Bandon Dunes, four hours south of Portland, is different. It makes no effort to be like anything other than Bandon Dunes. You can go expecting a taste of the old-world courses, but that's not what you'll find. If there is more scenic beauty in American golf, I haven't come across it.

NOTES

. . . .

. . . .

. . . .

. . . .

❑ **BANDON DUNES GOLF RESORT** Date:. . . . .

BIG CEDAR LODGE

The most famous hillbilly other than the Hatfields and McCoys struck it rich in the Ozark Mountains, and his kinfolk said, "Jed, move away from there." So, he moved to California. Johnny Morris struck it rich in the Ozarks and decided to stay, and golfers are thankful his kinfolk didn't make the same suggestion. The Bass Pro Shop founder didn't move to Beverly (Hills, that is). Instead, he poured some of his billions into grandeur and golf at the Big Cedar Lodge, where the luxury is the antithesis of the Clampetts' pre-oil-strike Ozark lifestyle.

Few who get into golf development have Morris's resources (*Forbes* estimates his wealth at $8 billion). He went out and got Tiger Woods to design the flagship course at Big Cedar Lodge. Payne's Valley is the first public-access course created by Woods's design firm, but all five of Morris's courses at the resort are so spectacular that in just a few years this wilderness resort in the United States' only rugged terrain between the Appalachians and the Rockies has become one of the world's best. Each course was built by a marquee designer and blends into the timberland here much more easily than the Clampetts blended into Beverly Hills. In addition to Woods, Jack Nicklaus, Tom Fazio, Ben Crenshaw, Bill Coore, and Gary Player have worked Morris's Ozark land into the marquee courses of Branson, Missouri, which has become known as one of Middle America's best golf destinations.

Morris began his road to fortune as a kid selling bait and tackle out of the back of his father's liquor store, and he's always been keen on connecting people with nature. Golf is one way, but so is fishing in the creeks and lakes deep in the Ozarks and a lengthy list of other outdoor activities. Indoors, Big Cedar is one of those opulent no-detail-overlooked places without being ostentatious. So, after a day on the courses, there is plenty of pampering to be done inside.

If golf were bubblin' crude, this would be the place to drill. Sit a spell, take your shoes off, and have a heapin' helpin' of Morris hospitality. Y'all come back now, y'hear?

NOTES

. . . .

. . . .

. . . .

. . . .

❏ **BIG CEDAR LODGE** Date:. . . . .

NORTHERN MICHIGAN

When a man buys a piece of land, with it comes the right to call it whatever he wants. So, if Everett Kircher wanted to call his 552-foot vertical drop a mountain, even though in the alpine world that's more of a molehill, then so be it. It was 1947 when Kircher bought his "mountain" in Northern Michigan for $1, giving it a place alongside the Louisiana Purchase and Manhattan as one of the greatest land deals of all time. He bought the mountain with the intent of introducing skiing to the area, and he did. In fact, Kircher became an innovator in the ski world, leading the way in snowmaking in the 1950s and in chairlifts over the next few decades.

But snow melts and skiing go dormant in the summer, even farther north than the frozen tundra of Green Bay. So Kircher climbed aboard his father's aging Ford farm tractor and tilled up a nine-hole golf course he called Hemlock. That sufficed for a while, but as interest in golf during Northern Michigan's short summers grew, the region needed more. Kircher built more at his Boyne Resort, which now includes 10 fine courses over three separate resorts. But others also recognized the opportunity, even if last call on the golf season is a couple weeks before Halloween. Golf exploded around the small town of Gaylord, where the Gaylord Golf Mecca includes Treetops Resort with its four great courses and one of the best par-3 courses in the country; four courses at Garland Lodge and Golf Resort, and two at Ostego Resort. Traverse City is the "Cherry Capital of the World," but the pickings for golf aren't too slim. Shanty Creek Resort has five courses, Grand Traverse Resort and Spa has three. The treat of Northern Michigan is Forest Dunes Golf Club, a 36-hole course built on sand dunes in the middle of the state.

The whole of Northern Michigan is knitted together by a plethora of small-town courses, some public, some private, but all wonderful experiences. The granddaddy of them all is the exclusive Crystal Downs Country Club, on a bereft piece of land between Lake Michigan and Crystal Lake. It may be nowheresville, but the course is ranked alongside Winged Foot Golf Club, Pebble Beach, Muirfield Village Golf Club, and Los Angeles Country Club. Don't turn down an invitation.

NOTES

. . . .

. . . .

. . . .

. . . .

❏ **NORTHERN MICHIGAN** Date: . . . .

ALABAMA'S ROBERT TRENT JONES GOLF TRAIL

Sometime in the late 1980s, David G. Bonner, CEO of the Retirement Systems of Alabama, had this outlandish idea to diversify the fund's assets by investing in golf. His thought, that investing in Alabama would mean a stronger Alabama retirement system. But golf?

What seemed like an off-the-deep-end idea wasn't just to build a golf course, but to build 378 holes of golf on eight sites across the state. And he didn't want to build them one at a time. So, sometime in the early 1990s a brigade of bulldozers started reshaping land around the Heart of Dixie into golf courses. Like many great innovators, he was ahead of his time. But if some slightly off-center guy in Iowa could build a baseball field to drive tourism, maybe golf could do the same thing for Alabama. And it did.

By the late 1990s golfers were pouring into the state to play golf on the Robert Trent Jones Golf Trail. These weren't run-of-the-mill layouts; they were designed by one of the game's great course designers on sites with spectacular terrain that appeared made for golf. And they were built to a scale beyond what was appropriate for the day, some stretching more than 8,000 yards. Golfers loved them, so they built more. Now, in the 384 miles between The Shoals in northwest Alabama and Lakewood Golf Club on Mobile Bay almost to the Gulf of Mexico, the unique trail of golf courses includes more than even Bonner imagined. There are 11 sites along the trail, some of which include hotels, luxury resorts, spas, restaurants, and residential developments. There are 26 courses (468 holes) on differing sites, each its own masterpiece carved from hills, valleys, marshes, and flatlands to provide a much wider variety of experiences than other destinations.

Some of the courses are named after geographical features, like the three at Hampton Cove (Highlands, River, and Short). Others make you wonder what you're getting yourself into—Fighting Joe and Schoolmaster at The Shoals or Mindbreaker, Heartbreaker, and Backbreaker at Silver Lakes. Others just pay tribute to their location, like the Legislator, Senator, and Judge courses of Capitol Hill just north of Montgomery.

More than half a million rounds are played every year on the trail, many by golfers outside Alabama, who spend their money not just on green fees but in hotels, restaurants, and shops. It all spurs Alabama's economy and ensures the state's pension fund will provide retirees everything it promises.

. . . .

. . . .

. . . .

. . . .

❏ **ALABAMA'S ROBERT TRENT JONES GOLF TRAIL** Date: . . . .

THE SOUTHWEST DESERT

After years of winging our way to Florida for the annual respite from the brutalities of a Northeastern winter, my aging group decided we were getting too old to constantly fight the wind and the threat of rain, meaning we'd have to hang around the hotel together (entirely unacceptable). The Sunshine State doesn't always live up to its billing in January. Someone suggested the desert. The flight is longer and the time change is annoying, but the courses have more geographic interest, with fairways lined by desert rather than the water and condominiums of Florida.

In the desert, maybe you can't remember your name, but you can certainly forget winter. That first year, we booked tickets to Palm Springs, which averages 350 days of sunshine each year. Streets in Palm Springs run due north-south or due east-west, sectioning the Coachella Valley into boxes like your Super Bowl betting grid. Some boxes are bigger winners than others. One square at the intersection of Frank Sinatra Drive and Bob Hope Drive contains Rancho Mirage Country Club. Another contains Desert Willow Golf Resort.

Many contain exclusive private clubs in this fashionable resort area that became a celebrity escape from Los Angeles. The squares start to fall apart as they nudge up to the Santa Rosa Mountains, and the golf gets even better at courses like Indian Wells Golf Resort and PGA West, an annual stop on the PGA Tour.

In case you haven't noticed flying over these states, the Southwest desert is vast, and though golf plays just a small role in it, there are many green oases. Scottsdale is a hotbed for trendy shops, restaurants, and upscale resorts where course designers have creatively used the desert as hazards between holes and as forced carries to get from fairway to green at outstanding courses like Greyhawk Golf Club, Quintero Golf Club, and We-Ko-Pa Golf Club.

Las Vegas is known for its nightlife, but there are plenty of daylight hours to idle away, and the golf can be awesome. Shadow Creek Golf Course and Wynn Golf Club are two of the most expensive courses in the world to play, and while they will be two of the best you will ever play, whether they're worth the price is up to you. There are plenty of more affordable courses around town and in other desert destinations like Mesquite, where courses like Falcon Ridge Golf Course and Wolf Creek Golf Club showcase the drama of the desert rolling right up to the edge of the playing surfaces.

The weather, scenery, outstanding courses—I've found many reasons to love desert golf.

NOTES

. . . .
. . . .
. . . .
. . . .

❏ **THE SOUTHWEST DESERT** Date:. . . . .

DESTINATION KOHLER

Had things gone slightly differently, the spectacular land alongside Lake Michigan that Pete Dye bulldozed into one of the country's greatest golf courses would be churning out nuclear power instead of triple bogeys. The property just north of Sheboygan was an abandoned airfield when Wisconsin Electric bought it in the 1970s and proposed the Haven Nuclear Power Plant. Local residents opposed the idea of generating great power along this great lake, and so the land's owner eventually gave up and sold the land to the Kohler Company, the iconic plumbing-products company founded by John Michael Kohler in 1873 that is still in the Kohler family.

It's hard to find a path from faucets to world-class golf, but Herbert Kohler, grandson of the founder, plumbed his way to a four-course destination. The marquee course, rugged and windswept Whistling Straits, has held two PGA Championships, the United States Golf Association (USGA) Senior Open and the Ryder Cup, making it one of just a few US courses open to the public on which the Ryder Cup has been played. The course is built along two miles of the Lake Michigan shoreline, exposing your shots to the sometimes-brutal weather that has caused more than 600 shipwrecks on the lake. It's sibling, the Irish Course, is a more manageable inland layout, another Dye design that while much less decorated is still a worthy resort course. The 36-hole Blackwolf Run property, which has twice hosted the US Women's Open, is also part of Destination Kohler.

More than just golf, the Kohler experience includes spas, fine dining, five-star hotels and remote cabins, and plenty of après-golf activities. But the draw is to play the Straits Course, which has taken down some of the best players in the world like a ship in a storm.

. . . .

. . . .

. . . .

. . . .

❏ **DESTINATION KOHLER** Date: . . . .

HAWAII: KAPALUA GOLF CLUB

If any of our states were a bucket-list destination—golf or otherwise— it would be Hawaii. Yes, it's overdone and over-commercialized, but isn't just about everything in golf?

The Plantation Course at Kapalua Golf Club is one of the country's best courses open to the public, and we see it every January on television, as the PGA Tour opens each season with the Tournament of Champions. Built on the slope of the 5,800-foot Pu'u Kukui mountain, we watch every year as drives roll down steep fairways for 25 seconds, ending up sometimes more than 400 yards from where they were struck.

The course was built in the early 1990s but often has the feel of a classic Northeastern layout. You'll never confuse it for that, as you'll spend much of the round gazing out over the blue Pacific hoping to catch a glimpse of a whale in the distance. There are plenty of downhill shots to make you feel like a big hitter. It's a big course with wide fairways to accommodate the wind and excessive roll, but there is still plenty of opportunity to hit a shot off the playing surface and into trouble among the trees and scrub brush of the craggy volcanic bluffs. Along the way you'll find a punchbowl green and bunkering that resembles early-US course architecture.

The Bay Course at the resort is a much more manageable challenge, but this is Hawaii. There are ocean beaches to bask on, cuisine to enjoy, whales to watch, and waterfalls to discover. And if you're the serious adventurer, you can venture up 10,000 feet to the summit of Mt. Haleakalā for the jaw-dropping beauty of the sunrise. But don't forget the golf.

NOTES

. . . .

. . . .

. . . .

. . . .

❑ **HAWAII: KAPALUA GOLF CLUB** Date: . . . .

CHAPTER 3

10 Tournaments You Should See

THE NATIONALISM OF THE RYDER CUP

Every two years the overtly civil and well-heeled game of golf takes on a Mr. Hyde–ish persona called the Ryder Cup. It is golf's single opportunity to step into the us-against-them arena of the Super Bowl or a collegiate national championship. During the polite clapping of a typical professional golf tournament, it can be difficult to determine who fans are rooting for. At the Ryder Cup there is no confusing the sing-song olé, olé, olé, olé for the passionate chant of USA, USA, USA. And you should be there to urge your side on.

The collegial antics of face-painting and color-coded attire that borders on the ridiculous goes beyond necessary to mandated—and this from otherwise well-mannered and established career-oriented citizens, not rabid student rowdies with an excuse to run wild. The first tee at a Ryder Cup is a sight to behold, and player introductions may not rise to the level of an NBA game, but they're about as close as you can get outside in broad daylight.

During the Ryder Cup, the current 12 best players from the United States play against the 12 best from the continent of Europe, strategizing their way around the course, not to win an individual tournament but to accumulate points in hopes of your team accounting for more points at the end than the opposing side.

The Ryder Cup started as a simple biannual exhibition match between professionals from opposite sides of the great water hazard (Atlantic Ocean) but has grown into one of sport's most dynamic events. Nothing in golf compares to the atmosphere of a Ryder Cup and very little in sports can equal it. For one long weekend every other September, the civility of the game takes a break. Although this is not what the Ryder Cup was intended to be in the beginning, it's way better.

NOTES

. . . .

. . . .

. . . .

. . . .

❏ **THE NATIONALISM OF THE RYDER CUP** Date:. . . . .

THE TRADITION OF THE MASTERS

"A Tradition Unlike Any Other." Indeed. The phrase is so ingrained in the golf lexicon that it is protected by trademark and used so often that golfers and nongolfers alike don't need to see the accompanying images of blooming azaleas at Augusta National to know the Masters is on the springtime horizon.

To the golfing world, the Masters represents more than a major tournament. Perhaps more so than the chirp of baby birds or the blossoms of a new season, the Masters is the manifestation of spring—the augur that golf's winter hibernation is at last over. When the spectacular greens and shades of pink have not yet returned to the winter-scarred tundra of my town, the images beaming from Georgia let me know that they are creeping their way north to percolate my course back from its winter blah-ness.

I watch the Masters on television, keeping an eye out the window to see if my grass has gotten any greener in the last hour. Only a lucky few obtain what might be the toughest ticket in sports. They get to peak in on the Wednesday par-3 contest and crowd around the first tee early on Thursday morning to watch the honorary starters, a tradition within "A Tradition Unlike Any Other."

Because the tournament is run by the club and not an overarching golf association, tickets are carefully controlled. The club offers patron badges (no one knows how many), which entitle the holder to pay the annual ticket price for access to the full week of the tournament for the holder's lifetime. By club rules, the badge can only be willed to a spouse. If the spouse declines, the badge is awarded to someone on the waiting list, which is so deep, Augusta National has only once since 1972 accepted new applications. There are also some tickets available through the club's lottery.

I'm happy watching on television. I can see all the crucial shots, though I can't experience any of the Masters traditions—no pimento cheese sandwiches, no watching players try to skip the ball off the pond onto the sixteenth green during practice rounds, no access to the reasonable prices of the merchandise tent. But at least at home I can keep an eye on the advancements of spring.

NOTES

. . . .

. . . .

. . . .

. . . .

❏ **THE TRADITION OF THE MASTERS** Date: . . . .

THE STRANGE, THE ODD, AND THE HISTORY OF THE OPEN CHAMPIONSHIP

Some of the best Indian food I've ever had was in St. Andrews. Yes, Scotland. By far my best Irish whiskey experience was at Bushmills near the small seaside town of Portrush in Northern Ireland. Somewhere there is a picture of me in full Scottish formalwear (kilt, knee socks, and classic ghillie brogue shoes) in front of the Turnberry Lighthouse, where earlier in the day I had stopped for a snack following the ninth hole of the Ailsa Course and realized that the Turnberry Golf Club employees who operate the halfway house have the best job in golf—serving snacks and light fare meals to golfers in a setting overlooking the jagged Ayshire coastline to the massive rock island Ailsa Craig 11 miles off shore in the Irish Sea. No other halfway house comes close to matching such beauty.

In the US, our national championship jumps largely from one major metropolitan area to the next without much distinction between the urban surroundings of the golf course. In Great Britain, the Open Championship is always played by the sea, in smallish towns steeped in millennia of history with buildings and records that date to the Middle Ages and sometimes to years with just three numbers instead of four.

When you cross the ocean to watch the Open Championship, it's a week lived differently. You're intoxicated by the aroma of malt wafting from the local fish and chips shop. You belly up to the bar in buildings that were standing before anyone even knew of America. You learn things about golf and about history. And you pick up on the local traditions and local knowledge, like the only half-joking saying at Turnberry that if you can't see Ailsa Craig, it's raining, and if you can see it, the rain just hasn't arrived yet.

The game is different on the famous links courses of Great Britain. It is played off the tight lies—where the grass isn't as plush in the sandy loam and the ball is nested closer to the ground—sometimes in excessive wind and rain, and sometimes on summer days that require a knit cap and a good base layer. Another bit of local knowledge: How do you recognize a newbie to British Isles links golf? They think an umbrella will help. It's always fun to watch the pros on TV struggling against the rugged elements of this part of the world. Maybe you'll get a taste of it when you're walking the fairways watching them.

NOTES

. . . .
. . . .
. . . .
. . . .

❏ **THE STRANGE, THE ODD, AND THE HISTORY OF THE OPEN CHAMPIONSHIP** Date: . . . .

SUPPORT YOUR LOCAL TOUR EVENT

I remember when the PGA Senior Tour created a tournament in my town. This was back when the Senior Tour was just beginning and greats like Arnold Palmer and Gary Player came to town, but not Jack Nicklaus. He was still too young. My oldest daughter was barely out of toddlerhood, and she and I went and spent the day watching. It was her introduction to golf, other than the plastic clubs and balls grandparents give as Christmas gifts to children of a golfer. She couldn't have cared less about the golf but thought walking the course and grabbing a hot dog for lunch with her old man was pretty cool. And I thought so, too.

The event lasted only a couple of years, but then the regular PGA Tour came to town. My daughter was old enough by then to say she'd rather go roller-skating with her friends than watch grown men chase a ball around, so I'd go by with friends. I'm not a big fan of watching others play golf, especially when I could be playing myself, but there's sort of an unwritten commitment that a golfer should support local golf events.

For a few years a Ladies Professional Golf Association (LPGA) Tour major came to my town. By then I had two girls, so we made it a threesome and enjoyed being able to get close enough to the ladies that they would pat the girls on the head and thank them for coming out to watch.

Eventually the USGA, recognizing my town really supported the local event, brought the US Open there—twice. It had been in town before, but back in the days of black-and-white photographs before television coverage existed and when great writers would bring the nuances of the event into your home via newspapers and monthly magazines.

But then the tour left. The majors left and aren't yet on any schedule to return. It's a shame that a market the size of my city no longer has a professional golf event. I miss it. Maybe I am a fan of watching others play golf.

· ·

· ·

· ·

· ·

❑ **SUPPORT YOUR LOCAL TOUR EVENT** Date:· ·

PARTY AT NO. 16 AT THE WASTE MANAGEMENT

In the button-down world of the PGA Tour there seems to be little room for anything except the norm. Players address their shot, the crowd goes silent, and even the softest of chirps from the gallery cause an interruption and reset. Really? You're making millions of dollars and you can't do your job unless there's complete silence? And that's what makes watching the sixteenth hole at the Waste Management Phoenix Open so cool. An otherwise mundane event in the otherwise mundane world of touring professional golf, the sixteenth at the Tournament Players Club in Scottsdale has become golf's biggest party scene, the antithesis of what tournament golf on this level has evolved to.

The hole is ringed by stadium bleachers, golf's Flavian Amphitheatre with polo-clad gladiators entering to fire a single shot under the glare and antics of drunken spectators more often hoping to see warriors crumble under the pressure so they can shout out their scripted cat calls. It is unlikely you'll find a more alcohol-infused scene at a college bar or a Super Bowl tailgate party than at the sixteenth at the Waste Management.

Silence and polite applause is unacceptable in the stadium of the sixteenth. Such inappropriate conduct is likely to get you thrown out of the place to make room for one more legitimate beer-swilling rowdy willing to hassle a player for any less-than-competent shot. The tournament leans in to its status as the rowdiest on the professional circuit and most players are happy to partake—or at a minimum accept—the antics. There are plenty of crazies, searing zingers shouted at the players, and alcohol—always much alcohol. The Waste Management tournament has done some awesome things for charity, and the party at the sixteenth has helped contribute to the generosity. But the more appropriate name for this tournament might be the Wasted Management Phoenix Open.

NOTES

. . . .
. . . .
. . . .
. . . .

❏ **PARTY AT NO. 16 AT THE WASTE MANAGEMENT**

Date: . . . .

WATCH FOR DISASTER ON THE SEVENTEENTH AT SAWGRASS

The seventeenth in Ponte Vedra, Florida, is home of the Players Championship each March. With its illustrious field of only the current best players in the world, this event equals the four majors in defining buttoned-down. The horseplay of Phoenix has no place at the prim-and-proper Tournament Players Club at Sawgrass, where at the classy Pete Dye design and the elegant Sawgrass Marriott Golf Resort and Spa not a blade of grass or a single oyster fork is out of place.

The famous island green of the seventeenth hole is so fiendishly designed and so devilishly placed that if golf has a hell, this might be it. Not only do mere rounds die here, dreams die here. There was the descension of Sergio Garcia, who came to this little piece of 150-yard purgatory in 2013 leading one of the most coveted tournaments in the world by a shot and dumped two balls in the water. Thanks for playing.

We view the seventeenth at Sawgrass like NASCAR fans might view turn four at Daytona. They want to see cool things happen, but if there's a six-car pileup somewhere along the way, that's just an added bonus. So, we camp out on the seventeenth knowing that at some point, someone is going to crash and burn. And, somehow, we don't sympathize with those who do. Instead, we smile contently because these great players have managed to lower themselves to our level, albeit just for one shot. They may be four-under par playing one of the most difficult courses in the world while we would be a million over par, but by misjudging the yardage or the elements, they manage to show the same blundering incompetence that we show on such a shot. And that's why we watch—because it's one of the few times the handicapped public golfer can relate to the professional golfer.

NOTES

....
....
....
....

❏ **WATCH FOR DISASTER ON THE SEVENTEENTH AT SAWGRASS**

    Date:..

THE PAST AND PRESENT OF THE US OPEN

When Tiger Woods was a young pro and my son was a beginning golfer, the US Open came to our city. Tiger had won the Masters and talk swirled about the possibility of him winning a consecutive major and perhaps going on to collect the modern Grand Slam, an unaccomplished feat that in Tiger's early years seemed like a reasonable possibility for him. His less-than-stellar first two rounds put that talk to rest but didn't keep him from making the cut. So, my son and I went out for the weekend rounds to follow Tiger, like everyone else in those days. Jack Nicklaus, in his late fifties, was playing in one of his final US Opens so the juxtaposition of the past and the future was a rare opportunity.

Few are able to play to the US Open level so late in their careers, so it's not often a weekend like this comes around. Not yet a teenager, my son, like all golfers his age, was fixated on Tiger, so we added ourselves to the tremendous gallery of spectators for much of the day. But I insisted we watch Nicklaus for his last three holes on Sunday because there was a chance this would be his final appearance in the national championship he had won four times. Nicklaus still drew a sizable gallery of his own, but it was nothing compared to the shoulder-to-shoulder, seven-or-eight-deep Tiger gallery of his early years. There are many things to see at the US Open besides the winner or the most popular players. Our national championship brings out the best in many lesser-known players.

Types of Shots

Ace: A hole in one.

Fade: A good shot that moves slightly from left to right.

Draw: A good shot that moves slightly from right to left.

Slice: A bad shot that curves from left to right.

Gimmie: A putt that is conceded by another player or just accepted as if it were holed.

Hook: A bad shot that curves from right to left.

Mulligan: A second shot taken as if the first shot was never hit.

Nutted: A shot hit as well as the player hitting can possibly do.

Snap hook: Worse than a hook.

Stripe: A well-struck shot.

X: A score of too many strokes to count on a single hole.

There's often a journeyman type who gets hot in the first round and climbs up the leaderboard. Occasionally, but very rarely, they stay there. As an example, there is Andy North, who won just three PGA Tour events but two of them were the US Open. Still, for every Andy North there is a T. C. Chen, who famously double-hit a chip shot, which handed the 1985 US Open victory to North. Or there's a star player who doesn't get the job done, like Sam Snead, who notably thought he needed a birdie on the last to win the 1939 US Open so he played aggressively—too aggressively. He made a triple bogey when really all he really needed was par to win. And, of course, there's Phil Mickelson's epic collapse on the eighteenth at Winged Foot in 2006 when he needed just a par to win and made double bogey.

You never know what you might see at our national championship. It may be history, or it may be career-scarring disaster, but it's always worth the price.

NOTES

. . . .

. . . .

. . . .

. . . .

❏ **THE PAST AND PRESENT OF THE US OPEN** Date: . . . .

THE PURITY OF THE US AMATEUR

In the era when great amateur players like Bobby Jones and Francis Ouimet wrote storybook endings from the fairways and exposed the country's masses to this strange game imported from Scotland, the amateur was at the top of the golf hierarchy. Professionals were more second-class golfers, often viewed as partaking in one big gambling game. As is often the case, money changed that, and now with all the great professionals, we tend to think of the contingent of golfers who play the game simply for the purity of it as "just amateurs."

We tend to overlook the fact that all great professionals start as amateurs, although in their rush to play for pay they might not focus quite as intently on the major amateur events like the US and British amateurs the way Jones and Ouimet did. Money drives the game these days, and the best amateurs are eager to get to the rewards of the professional rank. No recent career amateur has achieved the level of success or admiration of Jones, Ouimet, or the great English amateur John Ball, Jr., all of whom played in the time before the modern PGA Tour existed when the two national amateur competitions were among golf's four major events.

But watching the top amateurs offers views of high-level golf from the best vantage point for the smallest ticket price. One year at the US Amateur Championship I walked several holes within a few feet of the eventual winner, getting a close-up view not only of his shots but how he went about preparing for each shot, something not possible at any professional event.

The Havemeyer Trophy, awarded to the winner of the US Amateur each year, remains one of golf's most coveted prizes, even though it is not accompanied by a huge check of the game's professional tournaments that have less-sought-after trophies.

NOTES

. . . .

. . . .

. . . .

. . . .

❏ **THE PURITY OF THE US AMATEUR** Date:. . . . .

THE PRIDE OF THE PRESIDENTS CUP

The first tee at a Presidents Cup is a rare scene in golf. Grass-level corporate boxes with horseshoe-shaped stadium seating for 2,000 or more rising above the boxes provides a mini-college-football-like atmosphere. Players walk through a tunnel and appear on the first tee to be introduced and cheered on by fans from around the world. The exuberant atmosphere flows out onto the course, nudging toward but never quite getting to the level of sports rivalry. After all, most of the fans are well past their rambunctious college years.

US Presidents Cup opponents are players from around the world. Galleries are a melting pot of nations that come together in a united goal of winning a cup, without pay or the continental pride of the Ryder Cup to spur them on. One of the great things about the Presidents Cup is you could be side by side with fans from South Korea one hole, Japan the next, South Africa the next, and then Canada.

Occasionally, a player from a country like Fiji, Zimbabwe, or Taiwan (Chinese Taipei) represents the international team, bringing fans from their home countries.

Almost any given professional event has a similar collection of nationalities, but never are they all united in that one goal.

NOTES

. . . .

. . . .

. . . .

. . . .

❏ **THE PRIDE OF THE PRESIDENTS CUP** Date: . . . .

YOUR STATE AMATEUR

Golf was certainly not corrupted by money, at least no more than any other sport. But never believe a well-off professional golfer who says they don't care about the money, that they'd play for nothing. It's insulting to the people who have nothing.

If you want to see good golfers who actually are playing for nothing but the purity of the game and the intoxication of the competition, you'll find the best of your area at your state amateur tournament. These players really are out there for the love of the game. They're carrying their own bags, figuring it out as they go, often on courses unfamiliar to them, with no one other than maybe their girlfriends or parents watching. These are players who had to take vacation days from their real job to play in a golf tournament and are happy to do so because they love the game. They love the competition. Your state amateur tournament, and your state open, although there is a little money involved there, aren't just another stop on the tour, another way to meet expenses and pad a bank account. State amateur tournaments are as pure as tournament golf gets anymore.

NOTES

. . . .
. . . .
. . . .
. . . .

❏ **YOUR STATE AMATEUR** Date: . . . .

CHAPTER 4

10 Habits You Should Practice

PLAY BY THE RULES OF GOLF

If golf is such a game of integrity, why do we run roughshod over the rule book as if it were the US tax code? We bend, stretch, and outright break the rules that govern our sport without regard. We take deductions we know we are not entitled to: mulligans, do-overs, gimmies. We play on because what does it matter to the massive game if we paid a little less than we owed? The truth is that the kids playing pick-up basketball at the neighborhood playground court follow the rules of their game far more righteously than most golfers follow the rules of our game. If a foot is on the line when a three-point shot is taken, players on both squads see it and make sure the made basket counts two points and not three. Many a golfer, on the other hand, whose wayward tee shot rolls ever so slightly across the out of-bounds line, feels entitled to nudge it back onto the course and play on as if the rules make an exception for shots that end up inches out of bounds rather than more significant distances.

For some reason, in golf we tend to treat the rules more as guidelines. The United States Golf Association and Great Britain's Royal and Ancient Golf Club have put centuries into refining the rules of our game, and yet we treat them like speed-limit signs; yeah, we should do what they say, but if we don't get caught, are we really doing anything wrong? When you take a mulligan on the first tee or any tee, it's a victimless crime but a crime nonetheless.

At my club we've started making an allowance for balls that end up in divots in the fairway. You may nurse them back to a healthy lie. But the fundamental tenets of the game say play the course as you find it and play the ball as it lies. By what authority do we make the decision to disregard that particular rule, other than to say that as long as everybody is doing it, then the egregiousness is acceptable. But, amortized from golf to life, doesn't such action equate to anarchy?

In a game rarely played competitively, in which comradery outweighs the desire for proficiency in most foursomes, there is no need to be a stickler for the rules, except for that little thing called integrity. How often have we heard that golf is a game of integrity? Is it? I am always competitive with myself and have a need to constantly measure my level of success, which is not possible by playing loose with the rules. If all other players started looking at golf that way, then, maybe one day, we'll play our game as purely as those playground kids play theirs.

NOTES

. . . .

. . . .

. . . .

. . . .

❏ **PLAY BY THE RULES OF GOLF** Date: . . . .

QUIT WHINING

Golfers are whiners. I have no historical evidence or scientific data for this, but my guess is that we, as a breed, have been whiners and complainers since the very first bad bounce that resulted in a shepherd losing his ball in knee-high heather. In 1913 pros playing in the Open Championship complained about slow play when one round took a scandalous 3 hours and 10 minutes. You know what players today would do if golf could be played in 3:10? They'd complain, "I can't play when I'm rushing."

We whine in March that it's too cold. In April that it's too windy. In July that it's too hot. We whine that the greens are too hard. The greens are too soft. The rough is too thick. The rough is all burned out. Geez, doesn't anyone around here replace their divots? Why can't the superintendent do something about all these ball marks? As a breed, golfers are never happy. I'm not sure I've ever played a round of golf in which someone hasn't whined about something. In fact, I know I've never played a round where someone hasn't whined because I'm a whiner.

Mostly, I whine about my own lack of competence. I'm not saying my brand of whining is any less annoying than anyone else's, but I'm at least taking responsibility for my own incompetence. I have a very occasional playing partner whom I call Eeyore. I'm sure you know Eeyore—the golf world is against him, nothing ever goes his way, and nothing is ever his fault. A. A. Milne spins his character into a pessimistic and anhedonic but entirely lovable old gray donkey, but my Eeyore is just an ass.

He drones on and on about the poor design of the hole he just tripled, even when everyone else knows it is perfectly adequate, if not excellent, design work. Once Eeyore shot one-under on the front nine and was happy as Pooh in a honey pot with—shockingly—nothing negative to say about anything, even though he talked constantly. During his 43 on the back nine—true to character—Eeyore complained continuously about tricked-up pin placements, divots in the fairways, the sun being in his eyes. Finally, on the fifteenth hole, when he complained for the umpteenth time about how bad the greens on the backside were, I pointed out that the fifteenth green is within spitting distance of the seventh green, which he might take notice is on the front nine, and that since the two nines intertwine it would be almost an agronomic impossibility for the front nine greens to be great and the back nine greens to be terrible. Unable to shut him up with sound reason, he found other things to whine about all the way to the clubhouse.

Look, golf is a frustrating endeavor. You knew that when you signed up. There is quite an inventory of complaints to be made about in this game, but only a few have any scholastic merit. Grumble and grouse about the rest and it only makes you look like Eeyore—a total ass. Golf even has a nifty name for all the luck—good and bad—that it dishes out: "rub of the green." Enjoy the good, accept the bad, and deal with both—preferably in silence.

NOTES

. . . .

. . . .

. . . .

. . . .

❏ **QUIT WHINING** Date: . . . .

PUTT ALL YOUR THREE FOOTERS

In the casualness of our game and the comradery of a round, we tend to overlook one important thing—finishing the task. Our inclination often is to get the ball close enough to the hole to consider the job done, although in the real world of golf, as we all know, the ball needs to drop over the edge and into the hole, and only after that happens is the job complete and we can accurately account our fortune, or misfortune, in the appropriate box on the scorecard. But because the game is played in foursomes of friends, we treat the last few feet as optional. "That's good," we say because we are friends, and we don't want to offend anyone by challenging them to actually hole a putt. I don't think you would mow your grass or paint the living room wall and leave the last few feet unfinished. There is a necessity, a beauty, to finishing the job. So why should golf be any different?

A bumper sticker I once saw read: "The longest yard is a three-foot putt." I chuckled before I realized there was deeper meaning to it. We don't always do the work required. We don't always finish the job. Three feet seems simple enough, so we take it for granted; assume the distance is so easily negotiated that we don't bother with it. But ask any football coach facing fourth and goal from the one-yard line with the outcome of the game hanging in the balance, and I bet three feet looks more like three time zones. In golf, where players hit the ball 300 yards with one swing, three feet is insignificant until you have to cover it with one stroke of the putter and the only acceptable result is to watch the ball fall off the face of the earth. It's not that easy. Try playing a round, or a month, or an entire season putting all of your three-footers, and I think you'll agree.

A lot can happen in three feet—a little break, a little grain, imperfections in the green, old ball marks, a bug wandering aimlessly. A recent rules change allows us to tap down all the imperfections between our ball and the hole, but that hasn't seemed to do anything to help our enthusiasm to putt our three-footers.

The reason the three-footer is so hard has nothing to do with anything other than the fact that everyone, even your grandma in combat boots, should be able to make a three-foot putt. Yet even the best putters miss them. Even at the highest levels of golf like the Ryder Cup, three-footers aren't often conceded. But our everyday games are casual, so we don't care too much about three-footers because it's just three damn feet. A golf ball needs just six and a half revolutions to go three feet. I measured it once when I tired of hitting my three-foot putts six-and-a-quarter revolutions.

Many things in life look a lot easier than they actually are—until you have to do them.

NOTES

. . . .

. . . .

. . . .

. . . .

❏ **PUTT ALL YOUR THREE FOOTERS** Date:. . . . .

P(L)AY IT FORWARD

Most of us who play this game somewhat seriously have achieved some level of success in our non-golfing lives, or at least something that can monetarily be defined as success. The game is expensive and it takes time, two things not everyone has. My father—with six kids and a federal government paycheck—had neither. But he did play before we came along, and he left his old imitation hickory-shaft clubs in the basement hoping to get back to them one day. They collected dust and cobwebs until his four sons became curious about them. Golf, to me and my brothers in our youth, was whacking a Wiffle ball around in the backyard until we got bored of that and started whacking the Wiffle ball at each other. When the Wiffle ball sailed over the fence into Mr. Pipenbrink's yard, we turned the clubs around and pretended they were rifles and shot at each other. This was the 1970s, when parents didn't cringe at such behavior.

When I graduated from college and had some disposable income, I put some of it toward a set of Sam Snead Wilson Blue Ridge irons. I played in Converse Chuck Taylors with those circa 1950 clubs from my father's basement and couldn't break 100 without a few mulligans and lengthy gimmies. But I stayed with it and by the time I had a family was a respectable single-digit handicap with a club to call home. My club was not one of those blueblood, old-money clubs of which there are many surrounding my city and every city in the Northeast, where I live, and across the country. Members at my club include a high school principal, a grocery store manager, a bunch of mid-level managers, and even an aging writer who has somehow managed to make a living stringing words like these together for various articles and books.

So, technically, my kids grew up as country clubbers, although not the children of the well-heeled who belonged to the nearby hoity-toity clubs with amenities like squash or shrimp cocktail. The summer afternoon rounds when I introduced my kids to the game were followed by burgers and brats and maybe occasionally the club's "chef" would get creative and barbecue up some chicken on a Friday night.

The game has given me much, and sure, I introduced my kids to it and am now enthusiastically helping to introduce my grandkids to golf. But I'm not sure I'd be comfortable saying I've done my part to pass the game on to future generations. I could have done more. One of my friends, a couple of generations behind me, is at the club one evening every week during the summer organizing a junior program. He's one of the best players I've ever played with on a regular basis, and he's giving up time that could be spent practicing for his next big amateur tournament to keep 20 or so pre-teens herded and focused on chipping or putting or whatever the evening's lesson might be.

Two of my three kids took to the game and still play. But that's not exactly spreading the news. My friend, on the other hand, will likely have many more converts than I, his megaphone much louder than my whisper. Historically, there have been no golf little leagues. The game has been passed down from father to son/daughter generically until recently. Now, programs like Youth on Course, PGA Junior League, and the First Tee are coaching juniors not only in the ways of golf but the ways of life. Still, someone has to introduce kids to those programs when most parents don't have the time, resources, or familiarity with the game. So, we need people like my friend, or, perhaps, you?

NOTES

· ·
· ·
· ·
· ·

❏ **P(L)AY IT FORWARD** Date: ·

PLAY OCCASIONALLY BY YOURSELF

You hint at your age when you say, "There was a time," but there was a time when I played probably a dozen rounds each year by myself—just me, my clubs, and my thoughts. Our game is best served in a social setting, shared among friends and compatriots. But the game does not cease to exist just because members of your regular foursome, or any foursome at all, are busy at the office, or on vacation, or in pursuit of goals more important than trying to shave another tenth of a point off their handicap.

In golf, but maybe not in many other life endeavors, the soloist is not an expression of loneliness but a rejoicing in solitude, a state in which one is almost free of time and space and relieved of the encumbrances that clutter and pressurize one's life. Time alone proffers the opportunity to explore yourself, to find your voice, even if it is a high draw you're searching for. When we hit that you're-working-on-my-last-nerve feeling that turns us into an irascible version of ourselves, we know the best cure is solitude. Golf is there for you.

To the uninitiated, playing solo is one of golf's bedraggled moments, viewed by the non-player as woebegone. I once played 36 holes solo in a light-but-nagging rain on a Saturday afternoon. I'm sure residents of the neighborhood that my course winds through stared questioningly through their sliding-glass doors when they caught a glimpse of me squish-squashing along, droplets rolling from my bucket hat. But the golfers among them wished they were me.

Other sports don't accommodate the singleton. You can shoot hoops by yourself on the playground. You can hit a tennis ball against that piece of green plywood hanging on the chain-link fence at the back of the court. But at best, that's just practice, just idling time while you wait for the real thing. Golf offers the singleton the whole enchilada, the actual game, complete with the joys of shots well executed, the sorrow of loathly intentions, and everything added up in the end, a real number that gauges a level of success or failure and reveals something about your status in the game at that particular moment.

Golf alone helps you clear your head of the week's accumulated clutter and think about nothing but trying to carve a high fade to a way-right pin on a 200-yard par 3. Golf is such an individual game that it only makes sense to play by yourself every once in a while. Alone, there is no obligatory chit-chat, no moral imperative to compliment someone else's good shot, and no requisite listening to a playing partner's troubles. Spare me the lurid specifics and your incessant bellyaching. Actually, you don't need to spare me because you're not here. I am playing solo, comfortable in my own company.

Back in the day, all those late afternoons as the moon worked the sun over the horizon, it would be just me. Bared to its essentials, that's what golf is. You. Alone. By yourself, even if you're there with three buddies, even if there are 150 other players on the course. This game, unlike any other, always boils down to just you—whether you're alone or not. And that's one of the things I love about the game.

I haven't played solo in more than a decade, and I find that to be a shame. For the most part, golf is a social activity with a date-like quality—you ask people to play, you make the arrangements, you look forward to the appointed time, and when it arrives, you are excited about the potential that lies in every little aspect. I still crave time alone, but these days, unfortunately, I rarely find it on the course.

NOTES

. . . .
. . . .
. . . .
. . . .

❏ **PLAY OCCASIONALLY BY YOURSELF** Date: . . . .

WALK WHEN YOU PLAY

Years ago, I read about a study in a prestigious medical journal finding that the human race is inherently lazy. I'd say that conclusion is rather obvious and not at all worthy of a prestigious medical journal, but the study takes an interesting look at why we are lazy. Apparently, we've evolved that way, no different than the way a collie has the urge to round up anything that moves.

Unknowingly, the study goes a long way to uncovering the problem with golf. Our sport goes against the ingrained genetics to be a civilization not of doers but of couch-sitters. If we're more willing to invest ourselves in watching football (or sitcoms or yet another season of *Survivor*) from the comfort of our Lazy Boy recliner than participate in golf—or apparently anything that might make us healthier—then aren't we condemned to a shorter and far less interesting existence?

We invest entire weekends in watching games or stories where the outcome makes absolutely no difference in our lives, when a good walk—whether we spoil it or not by our inept play—can enhance our being in many positive ways, from our hearts to our waistlines to our minds.

In support I tell you that Gene Sarazen lived to be 97; Byron Nelson, 94; Sam Snead died four days short of his ninetieth birthday; Arnold Palmer, 87; Ben Hogan, 84. Celebrity golfers seem to cross the finish line long after the scheduled arrival date of most celebrities.

Another study I read found that, ultimately, walking is the only exercise you need. Hmmm. Walking? Golf? Seems like a simple answer. When I walk my course it takes me about 14,000 steps (16,000 when I have to chase the ball farther off line than normal). So, if I walk on Saturday and Sunday, I get in more steps in two days than I would in a month of pacing the few steps between my desk, the couch, and the kitchen. I'm not saying golf is the answer to our nation's sedentary lifestyle, but the anecdotal evidence suggests it's a start.

NOTES

· ·

· ·

· ·

· ·

❑ **WALK WHEN YOU PLAY** Date: ·

KEEP A LEGITIMATE HANDICAP

In other more casual or amateur-level sports, there is no certain way to measure progress. If you're playing pick-up basketball and knock down three three-pointers in a game, you've done well. But if you miss three the next game, have you made any progress? Golf's World Handicap System (WHS) charts all of your scores (assuming you appropriately record them) and reports your progress on the first and fifteenth of every month. If you're an 11 handicap on the first and a 10 on the fifteenth, you take pride that you're progressing in a positive direction.

In golf, each stroke counts and each round's score matters. In a theoretical golf world, every player would input each of their exact scores into the system, which then applies its algorithm and calculates every player's handicap not as a simple average of their scores but as an indication of their potential. The system is quite complex, as it relates every score you shoot to the difficulty of the course and even the weather conditions of the day. But the sad fact is, few golfers maintain a handicap. And the sadder fact is that many golfers who do, manipulate the system to their advantage. The United States Golf Association says there are about 26 million golfers, but only about 12 percent of them participate in the handicap system. Yet it's the handicap system that makes golf objective. Does that mean 88 percent of American golfers don't care about monitoring their progress? Do those 88 percent just muddle along in blind mediocrity or less? Golf challenges us in many ways, and to avoid noting one's progress, even if that progress is backwards at times, seems like you're not willing to put in the effort and accept the grade.

The handicap is the foundation of our game. It allows everyone to play as equals even though everyone is far from equal. But the handicap system is abused more often than golf's rule book. Who among us has not at times conveniently forgotten to enter a particularly good score, knowing that it will bring our comfortable 7.5 handicap index down to 6.8 and mean you're given one less stroke in next weekend's money game? There's always a little scratch or some pro shop gift certificates on the line, and we adjust our chances of winning by massaging our handicap to a number we know we can play to regularly and not just on those rounds that we play to our potential. The WHS allows everyone to play equitably regardless of ability, which is what makes golf unique—higher handicap players can compete side-by-side with better players so that friends can all share the comradery the game affords regardless of ability.

But the system relies on the integrity of all players, and golfers seem to prove daily that their integrity matches that of a Washington politician. We manipulate the truth, withhold information, devise alternative facts, or just plain forget. Washington politicians care nothing about what's good for all but only about establishing footing for the next election. Golfers care not about the game as a whole, only about establishing a handicap that will give them the best chance of winning some pro shop certificates in the next tournament.

One summer at my club the same golfer won six net events and blatantly didn't post any of the scores in the WHS but somehow remembered to post each of his bad scores throughout the season. He was run out of the club but reigns as the example of why the World Handicap System, as good as it is in theory, can't legislate integrity. The quality of its calculated handicaps is determined by the quality of the players inputting information. You know, garbage in, garbage out.

NOTES

. . . .

. . . .

. . . .

. . . .

❏ **KEEP A LEGITIMATE HANDICAP** Date: . . . .

TAKE A LESSON

I've been having these moments of clarity lately that are both exhilarating and exasperating. At times these days, the game has never come so naturally. The haze that has been my golf swing for 40 years now clears and I can envision not only the end result of each shot but the path by which to get there. And I can actually follow that path to make shots happen on a regular basis. This clarity is not so focused that I can hit a high draw or a low fade on demand, just clear enough that I can execute the game at my level of mediocrity.

My authentic golf swing, as the legendary-though-fictional seer Bagger Vance would call it, is sort of an outside-in, over-the-top swipe at the ball, similar to what a samurai warrior might use to behead an enemy fighter. It's an athletic move but certainly not one ideal for projecting a golf ball down a narrow fairway then onto a green.

I've struggled against that swing for decades with about the same success I would have in attacking with my 9-iron a samurai warrior intent on beheading me. This new era of my golf swing, which has most importantly brought about a comfortable consistency, is coming from a series of lessons with my pro.

My pro is teaching me a more modern golf swing. He says I need to get my hips more level and closer to the ball so I can create the space by turning my right hip farther away from the ball on the backswing and my left hip entirely behind me by straightening my left leg on the through swing. The feeling he's trying to get me to is almost that of walking backwards.

It feels awkward, but it produces these moments of clarity where I not only understand what I'm trying to do, but I know I am going to do it. I've given up chasing distance, and I recognize that I'll never be a great putter. But maybe late in my career I can re-address some of the basics, even if those basics are quite different from the ones I was taught when I picked up this game.

So, I'm running with it. Perhaps these moments of clarity become woven into my game; perhaps they are just occasional awakenings no different from those that have appeared and disappeared during the last four decades. Give me another four decades and I should have the game figured out.

. . . .

. . . .

. . . .

. . . .

❑ **TAKE A LESSON** Date: . . . .

STAY CONNECTED TO YOUR YOUTH

One of my favorite rounds of the year is an annual get-together with three high school buddies whom I see only this one time each year and only because we get together to play this one round of golf at the muni in the town where we grew up. Our annual day of beer and revelry usually goes down around Memorial Day, in that brief window after the aeration holes heal but before the summer heat turns unkempt municipal fairways the color and texture of Rice Krispies. The only purpose golf serves is to keep us coming home each year, because, quite frankly, the four of us have so little in common anymore beyond the game that I can't imagine another scenario where we would willingly hang out.

Love may keep twosomes together, but it's golf that keeps foursomes from straying. Through golf, the four of us do what long-lost buddies do—recount our glory days, which for this group is mostly teenage inanity from the "old neighborhood." In fact, this day is the only golf day of the year when there is no dissection of golf shots gone awry or nineteenth-hole conversations about drained 40-footers. Even the quality shots go largely unnoticed as they come amidst stories of past capers and cavorting and memories of largely harmless mischief that 40 years on reflects as more juvenile doltishness than the grandly planned and humorously executed escapades we thought they were at the time.

In our salad days we viewed golf as an adult activity. Our youthful tastes ran to sports that involved collisions or, minimally, objects that actually moved as we tried to hit them. There was no time to chase a little white ball around a cow pasture. We had real sports to play and real mischief to get into, like plotting revenge on Mr. Pipenbrink for extending his garden into the neighborhood common area, thus commandeering a chunk of our third-base line in the name of tomatoes, cucumbers, and leaf lettuce.

While the country club kids were taking golf seriously and playing in tournaments where juniors could break 80, the boys from my side of the tracks were sneaking onto the local muni through the hole in the chain-link fence near the seventh green—until the crabby old pro the adults called Smitty, and we called much worse, caught on to us. He had a city maintenance crew patch the hole, derailing our youthful progress toward winning The Masters or the US Open because $3.25 to play 18 holes was too sizable a sum to extract from an allowance of two bits a week and whatever we could scrape together cutting lawns and shoveling sidewalks. That money had to go for more important things like underage beer or fuel for the car in case we lucked into a Friday night date.

Back then, we didn't know a good course from a bad one, but now we realize our neighborhood course was the definition of a dog track. Built without much thought as to where tees and greens should be placed or how to build either to any sort of agronomic standard, the course served the purpose for which it was intended: to provide cheap recreation to town residents. The town golf course was no different from the town swimming pool or the town playground or the town band shell, where on Sunday nights Polkaman Jack and the Jolley Aces would play and adults would gather to talk about grown-up things like the PTA or complain about their bosses or the mayor or their spouses.

To us, golf was tied to the lucre of capitalism, a game for bluebloods behind the gates and tall hedges of their private clubs. Others, like our fathers, who wanted to play once or twice each summer, lined up at the local muni in the ungodly hours of weekend mornings when only the third shift workers and the unscrupulous were about, hoping they'd get a starting time early enough that they might be home in time to do a little yard work before dinner.

Today, golf is a game of the people—perhaps the true American pastime—readily available to everyone. You don't have to be a country clubber to enjoy a great course in outstanding condition. Unlike the limited choice of courses our non-country-club fathers had, golf is a smorgasbord of options for our annual round. But for this one day my high school cohorts and I prefer the baked course Smitty used to chase us off of, the one that hasn't changed much in the last 40 years; the one with the sprinkler head in the first green; the one where the posted dress code is simply "shirt and shoes required," with no mention of collars or even pants. The tee time policy is "first come, first served," and there is always someone wanting to be served.

Over the years there have been umpteen proposals to close down my town course and turn the fairways into cul-de-sacs lined with three-bedroom, two-and-a-half bath domains. But the regulars, the generations that have followed my father and his buddies, have fought off would-be developers, claiming quite rightfully that the course is a living, breathing part of the town's history and therefore a part of their own histories. I fear that eventually this course where my friends and I introduced ourselves to the game in a twice-a-summer whirl of whiffs and shanks and running from Smitty will succumb. Someone will come along with enough money and an offer too good to refuse. But I would hate to see the place plowed. The older we get, the fewer things remain to connect us to our insouciant youth. The shabby town muni, this one and all the others that still exist, their unkempt and unshaven selves, still have a place in this game. Every dog track has its day, and for me, this particular dog track has had many—with hopefully more to come.

NOTES

. . . .

. . . .

. . . .

. . . .

❏ **STAY CONNECTED TO YOUR YOUTH** Date:. . . . .

GO OUT ON TOP

"We'll always have Paris," Rick says to Ilsa as he convinces her to get on the plane for Lisbon. But he is staying behind, not because he doesn't want to pay the checked baggage fee but because he knows their lives will be better apart, that they will never recapture the magic of the city where they fell in love.

Golf is full of *Casablanca* moments, exhilarating highs that we meet and fall in love with and that—like Paris—are both hard to forget and impossible to maintain. A 9-handicap friend once shot 71. If ever there was a time to say, "We'll always have Paris," and get on the plane, that was it. We all encounter those moments—our chance to grab a blank letter of transit, fill in our name, and leave the game for a new world. But in golf, as in Casablanca, only a fortunate few make it out. The rest of us remain in the purgatory of the game. And wait and wait and wait.

My 9-handicap friend will never do better than 71, but he didn't get on the plane. The next day he was back in the abyss of the game and shot 87. We all cross those moments when, if we had the guts and good sense, we could go out on top. But only Bobby Jones recognized the opportunity for what it was when he retired after winning the Grand Slam in 1930. The rest of us hang around in this smoky gin joint of golf. If we were honest with ourselves, we would have to wonder what we see in a game that offers endless exasperation, is harder to figure out than differential calculus, and no matter how much we put into the relationship, we will spend almost all of our time in the despair of *Casablanca*, only hoping to recapture the fleeting moment of Paris. And at some point, we will probably regret not taking the opportunity to get on the plane. Maybe not today. Maybe not tomorrow, but soon and for the rest of your life.

It's just that the game holds these come-hither qualities that make us believe this is the beginning of a beautiful friendship. Like a Paris romance, the game is addictive. You work at it and hang on to the moments that make it special, but inevitably you have to wonder if things might not have been better had you Bogart-ed it and made a clean break. What might have been? I wonder—usually during a stretch of poor play—how much different my life would be had I at some point gotten on the plane.

We all know a guy who played one round of golf in his life and hated it so much that he never spoke of it again, as if he had witnessed the unspeakable realities of war. I kinda get it. More and more lately, I kinda wish I had been him after my first torturous round. The time, the money, the frustration—what does it all add up to? I think of the hours I've spent chasing Paris moments. Forget all the ancillary stuff, just the hours. Add them up—it's impossible—and think about what else they might have gone toward. You start to wonder what the game's opportunity cost has meant to your life—the money you might have saved, or earned, in the time spent chasing futility on the course; the other relationships you might have cultivated; the places you might have traveled to. In the end, I will probably never get to the actual city of Casablanca, but I can say, "Yeah, but I shot 65 back in 2008." Does that make it all worth it?

Types of Courses

Muni: A course owned by a governmental entity; often, but not always, a derogatory term.

Royal golf clubs: The title "Royal" is restricted to "institutions of eminence, long standing and secure financial position, and devoted to national, charitable, and scientific objects," according to Scott Macpherson's book *Golf's Royal Clubs Honoured by the British Royal Family 1833–2013*. The Royal title is generally given to a club with an elevated status with members who come from families of wealth and influence.

Links: A term for a course that plays mostly in the sandy loam next to an ocean.

One summer not long ago, a friend asked me to play in a two-man tournament and accidentally asked me for my handicap index as of April 15 instead of August 15. I went back and found that in those four months my handicap had changed by one-tenth of a point. So, I suppose what I'm wondering here is maybe it's time for me to get on the plane. What's the point of continuing on in unfluctuating mediocrity? My Paris moment was clearly that round of 65 in '08, but that's long gone. I didn't get on the plane. Now I've reached that age where maybe I should just cut it off in hopes of something greater. More time has passed since I played my best round ever than French refugees spent in Casablanca, and those times when I feel I still have that game in me are fewer and fewer. Yet I go on. Like a man who's trying to convince himself of something he doesn't believe in his heart.

In the end, like Rick and Ingrid Bergman's Ilsa, our romance with golf is doomed to end in heartache. Always heartache. One of us will escape the purgatory of Casablanca, but it won't be me. Waiting. Waiting. Waiting. I'll never get out of here. I'll die in Casablanca. Golf and I will forever be the tragic story of unrequited love. We will never reach that harmonic accord where we live happily ever after. Not even the wisdom of a cynical, mercenary drunkard—even if it is Humphrey Bogart—can make that happen.

And so, I wonder. Of all the gin joints in all the towns in all the world, why did I have to walk into golf. Oh, what the hell. Play it again, Sam.

NOTES

. . . .

. . . .

. . . .

. . . .

❏ **GO OUT ON TOP** Date: . . . .

CHAPTER 5

10 International Destinations You Need to Experience

ILL IRISH WINDS

I hate writing about the weather. As the great Irish writer and poet Oscar Wilde once opined: "Conversation about the weather is the last refuge of the unimaginative." But then, O. W. never tried to hold a 3-iron against an Irish wind on the seventh at Ballybunion, hoping not to rinse the shot in the adjacent North Atlantic. O. W. never needed to hit a driver into a 30-mile-per-hour wind, praying that it would somehow be enough club to reach the 236-yard and appropriately named "Calamity Corner" at Royal Portrush.

And so, he never had the ensuing nineteenth-hole conversation about *that* weather. He never relived the misadventures of golf in an Irish wind in a pub conversation that night or even some night many years later because these stories about Irish weather linger for years, and there is nothing unimaginative about those conversations.

I have been traveling to Ireland to loop its wonderful courses for decades now, and my trips are often daily footslogs through wind so strong it flaps your underwear, and rain—sometimes just a brief shower leading to an Irish rainbow, sometimes a driving angst that tests the limits of Gore-Tex—but always rain. The aficionado of links golf knows all too well that wind and golf is a collocation as necessary as Ireland and Guinness. Golf is not a sugar plum game here. It's hard—like tenth-grade calculus hard. For decades I've been traveling to wee Ballybunion, where the 2,000 or so residents are, quite rightfully so for enduring its weather, privy to many more pubs than churches. The town never changes and neither does the weather. I have been around this island a dozen times at least and covered almost every inch of its great courses, usually in weather far less hospitable than the Irish folks I've met along the way. But when you fly across an ocean to play golf, you don't not play. In Ireland over the years, I have:

- Huddled in a cleft of one of the large dunes surrounding the famous Dell Hole at Lahinch Golf Club seeking respite from the brutality of the wind, rain, and occasional sleet driving hard off the North Atlantic.

- Tried to gauge how far a full swing with the putter would bounce and roll my ball along the firm links terrain of Waterville Golf Links because hitting the ball in the air would only allow the Irish wind to molest it and drop it indignantly to the ground without regard as to its intended destination.

- Seriously, and I mean seriously, contemplated this offer from a gentleman driving by as I searched for my wind-blown, rain-soaked, and now astray Titleist in the spring-thickened heather to the right of Ballybunion's fifth fairway (almost the farthest point from the clubhouse and right at the edge of the town): "Sn-no dae fa galf, laddie. Be 'appy to drive ye bach ta da cloobhouse." I declined, only because my three companions, in their unique and somewhat perverted way of standing up to Irish weather, consider starting and finishing a round on a day of such ferocious wind and proverbial sideways rain some sort of badge of golf courage.

Personally, I prefer a warm, dry peat fire reflecting golden in a tumbler of Irish whiskey neat while dozing in an overstuffed chair in the hotel lobby to the rigor of golf in the worst weather the west coast of Ireland can deal. Call me a milksop, a namby-pamby, a crybaby, a wimp—all of which my friends would have on a day in 2010 had I not pried myself from the coziness of said peat fire to play on a day when the seagulls grounded themselves, the jackrabbits burrowed deep, and even the hearty Irish livestock took cover. We were the only foursome to play the course that day. Not another one of our group of eight Americans nor a single Ballybunion member dared.

Now, I say the following not to brag, but to try to define for you just how gruesome Irish links weather can be: I am a bit of an accomplished player, having shot 65 on two occasions and twice having been the medalist in my state amateur qualifying tournament. But on this atrocious day I played so hard on the monster, uphill eighteenth at Ballybunion against such a ferocious gale (the ball kept blowing off the tee until finally I just heeled up a clump of turf and hit three-wood off it) and incomprehensible rain because I needed to make a double bogey to avoid shooting 100. It was a most satisfying 99.

There have been many an Irish morning when I have woken to the locomotive-like whooshing and whistling of the wind forcing its way through tiny gaps in the windowpane of my hotel room, or rain not gently pitter-pattering against the window but splashing against the glass as if thrown up from a tire speeding through a puddle. I look out and say there's no way we can possibly play today. But we do. We always play.

Occasionally we get a snappy, blue-sky day when the wind isn't strong enough to ripple the Irish flag on the clubhouse pole. These days are rare in Ireland, and I consider them payback for all the Irish rain that has dribbled down my neck and soaked my clothes from the inside of my Gore-Tex; payback for all the dripping snot wiped from my nose with the back of my rain gloves; payback for all the inside-outted umbrellas; for all the hats and head covers blown to oblivion; for all the FootJoys carefully placed on the hotel radiator and dutifully turned on the hour in the hope that they would be dry by tee time tomorrow.

The southwest of Ireland is exposed to the expanse of the great Atlantic Ocean and the trade winds that cross its vastness, gathering steam and delivering their payload on great courses like Waterville, Tralee Golf Club, Lahinch, and Ballybunion. Occasionally the weather relents and a lustrous sun paints the green links of Ireland as nature intended—the Emerald Isle. Those rare magically delicious days are a scene that O. W. likely could have found the words to describe had he been willing to converse about the weather.

NOTES

. . . .
. . . .
. . . .
. . . .

❑ **ILL IRISH WINDS** Date: . . . .

THE OLD SOD

The couple from Connecticut sitting next to me at the bar in the Royal Golf Hotel Dornoch tells me how they and several friends have been coming to Dornoch for decades. We drink single-malt Scotch and compare notes. Eventually I ask what they think of Brora Golf Club and Golspie Golf Club, two fine but unknown links courses not far from Dornoch in the Scottish Highlands. They were on my itinerary earlier in the week of my first trip to the Scottish Highlands and I thoroughly enjoyed both.

"Never played them," comes the reply.

I'm taken aback. Royal Dornoch Golf Club, the golf course on the other side of the bar wall, is, make no mistake, one of the world's finest links. It is worthy of coming to Scotland over and over again to play. But being into their fifth decade traveling to Dornoch and not playing some of the other courses in the area is very much like visiting the Louvre and only looking at the Mona Lisa. Scotland is full of famous courses that are sacred ground where the game began centuries ago. But they are not the only ancient links that pushed the game along in the early days.

Scotland is dotted with courses that don't appear on anyone's list of the best courses in the world. There are no travel brochures luring golfers to places like Boat of Garten or Moray or Elie or Crail. The entire country is littered with rarely-heard-of links courses that have never held the Open Championship but are as much a part of the home of golf—some even more so—as some of the historic venues. In the small seaside burgh of Crail, not far from St. Andrew's, 11 gentlemen gathered in a local pub in 1786 and created the Crail Golfing Society, likely after playing a rudimentary form of the game for a number of years across the linksland near Crail. At the time, only six other golf clubs had been formed.

Yes, it is the lure of the Old Course and its compatriots on the Open rota that brings golfers from around the world, but golf has been played across the linksland near small Scottish towns for centuries now, and it is in those places where you find the essence of the Scottish game. The true character of the Scottish game—the places where you get the real picture of how golf was played in the early days—is found in outback towns like Brora, where the club that formed in 1891 still plays on the course largely as it was originally designed, or Peterhead, which dates to 1841.

A great trip to Scotland doesn't have to hinge on whether you can get a starting time at the Old Course, because in St. Andrews you're likely to get paired with an attorney from Chicago. But show up at the wonderful layout at Leven Links, just 10 miles south, and you're more likely to play with a haberdasher from Earlsferry or a pewterer from Anstruther. No golfing journey is complete without playing the great courses of Scotland. But no Scottish golf journey is complete without seeing the real history of the game at the country's lesser-known gems.

NOTES

. . . .

. . . .

. . . .

. . . .

❑ **THE OLD SOD** Date:. . . . .

ENGLAND'S MAGICAL HISTORY TOUR

Four mop-top musicians with a loud, electric sound that parents of the 1960s didn't care for but their children craved may have put Liverpool, England, on the map of musical history, but long before the Beatles, their hometown was a symbol of the greatness of Edwardian England. The Albert Dock was one of the world's great ports and has direct ties to the three worst maritime disasters—the *Titanic, Empress of Ireland*, and *Lusitania*—but for golfers who come here it is easy to overlook this history in favor of the greatest stretch of linksland golf in the British Isles. The courses in the 25-mile stretch from Liverpool to Lytham have hosted six Ryder Cups (including the first) and more than 30 Open Championships. Nowhere else in all the great golfing linksland of the British Isles is there as much high-caliber golf in such a condensed space.

A rudimentary form of the game has been played here for centuries, and the formalization of actual golf courses began during the reign of Queen Victoria. The three royals—Royal Liverpool Golf Club, Royal Birkdale Golf Club, and Royal Lytham and St. Anne's—are all regular venues for the Open Championship, but sewing them together are wonderful courses like Wallasey Golf Club, West Lancashire Golf Club, Formby Golf Club, Hillside Golf Club, and Southport and Ainsdale Golf Club, all crafty layouts well over 100 years old. The rawness of a pure links like West Lancashire, the understated elegance of Wallasey, the oddity of treelined holes on links courses like Hillside and Formby, and the history of Southport and Ainsdale, where the first Ryder Cup was played, leave little doubt that England's Golf Coast is beyond compare, as is its shipping history.

You may remember in the Hollywood interpretation of the sinking of the *Titanic* that Liverpool is written across the stern of the distressed ship as it plummets to the bottom of the Atlantic. The ship was built largely by Liverpudlians who worked for the White Star Shipping Line, then headquartered at the Royal Albert Dock. The *Lusitania*, the fastest ship crossing the Atlantic at the time, sailed from Liverpool to New York and on a return in voyage 1915 was torpedoed by the Germans during World War I. *Empress of Ireland*, a Liverpool-to-Canada liner, was broadsided in thick fog by a huge coal ship in the St. Lawrence River just four miles from shore in 1914.

Less than 30 years after these disasters, John, Paul, George, and Ringo were born in Liverpool, and their history is immortalized in Liverpool as well. You can walk down Penny Lane and find there still is a bank, a barbershop, and a shelter in the middle of the roundabout. You can stand at the red iron gate to Strawberry Field, the Salvation Army house where John played in the yard as a child. You can still have a pint at the Cavern Club, where the Beatles began to gain fame.

The Beatles weren't much for golf, so they never enjoyed the greatness of the game near their hometown.

. . . .

. . . .

. . . .

. . . .

❏ **ENGLAND'S MAGICAL HISTORY TOUR** Date: . . . .

WELSH MAGIC

There is a reason Wales is known as a great country for hiking adventures—because driving in the country is an adventure all its own. Wales is a country of country roads. Don't get me wrong, it's a wonderful country to drive around. Just don't plan on making a 50-mile trip between courses in an hour.

But that means on your golf trip to Wales you will see more than just fairways and greens. You'll pass through towns with names that start with a confounding double *L* followed by a collection of letters that would make an awful Scrabble rack. And you need a pronunciation guide to read a map. Some useful hints: The Welsh double *L* is pronounced like our single *L*, although you must force air across both sides of your tongue in making the sound. Their double *D* is roughly equivalent to our *th*. Their *C* is always as in "cat" or "kill" and never as in "city." And when in Harlech—and you will be—you must pronounce the first syllable with such a throaty rasp that it sounds like you're hacking up a fur ball.

You will need help with all of this, but no worries. The people of Wales are happy to see you. They understand Wales is the undiscovered country of the United Kingdom. Golfers from around the world know every Open Championship course in Scotland, England, and Northern Ireland, but few will know the intricacies of Royal Porthcawl Golf Club or the fact that Royal St. David's Golf Club plays across land naturally reclaimed from Irish Sea over centuries.

And if you don't know these courses, there is little hope you'll know a place like Pennard Golf Club, where on my first visit on the fourth tee box I stood grinding over the yardage book, glancing at the book then surveying the distance again and again and each time finding it impossible to calculate how one relates to the other. Then, as if by the grace of the Welsh golf gods, an elderly member playing another hole took pity on my befuddled soul.

"The fourth fairway goes down there." He pointed. "This over here is the ninth fairway. When you get to the dogleg, make sure you play to the green on the left. The green on the right is the eighteenth. Then tenth goes down there into the valley, and then it goes in and out and all around. It's quite a trip."

The whole of Wales is quite a trip. Everything is so natural, so rugged. At a wonderful course called Southerndown Golf Club, I had this uneasy feeling as I poked around in the head-high gorse to the left of the first fairway looking for my wayward Titleist. I was not too worried about the ball or the ensuing penalty stroke; it was more the set of eyes peering back at me that had me concerned. The sheep at Southerndown have a proprietary right to graze on the course. They have taken up residence in the gorse, clearing away the lower foliage of the bushes to create little caves of creature comfort, and they would rather you not stick a 3-iron into their living room while searching for your ball.

Places like these as well as the courses in towns like Tenby, Aberdovey, Ashburnham, and Conwy, and the shared course of the towns of Pyle and Kenfig are all natural and craggy, and if you're used to the clearly defined fairways and plush conditions of American golf, when you come to Wales, be prepared for ruggedness, tight lies, wind, rain, and hangovers. You'll love it like I do.

NOTES

. . . .
. . . .
. . . .
. . . .

❑ **WELSH MAGIC** Date: . . . .

NO TROUBLES IN NORTHERN IRELAND

If you don't understand the political structure of the British Isles, you might find it confusing that Northern Ireland shares the island with the Republic of Ireland, and you have to cross an international border to get from one Ireland to the other Ireland. The Troubles refers to the decades between the 1960s and late 1990s when Catholics who were pro-Irish nationalists and fought for the reunification of Ireland quarreled violently with Protestants who were pro-British and unionists, and who wanted to remain with the United Kingdom. A peace agreement in 1998 quelled the violence for the most part, but the two religions still live largely separate and segregated lives in the same country, which remains part of the United Kingdom.

Through it all, the age-old golf of the country has remained spectacular. On my first visit to Northern Ireland, the days of the dying embers of the religious strife, a minor religious protest had caused the military to take to some streets. I drove through checkpoints, around burning rubble in the streets, and with the help of the military, easily and comfortably made my way from Royal County Down Golf Club (RCD) to Royal Portrush Golf Club. Now when I visit, I don't know what religion the people I meet practice, but on the whole the people of Northern Ireland couldn't be more welcoming. Once, due to a delayed flight, three friends and I showed up for our tee time at Royal County Down with just minutes to spare. The pro told us, "Don't worry. Take your time. Look around the shop. We'll get you out when you're ready."

I have been awed by the rugged beauty and naturalness of RCD since my first tee shot there decades ago. Bunkers have been worn away by the wind and perhaps burrowing livestock so deeply that the dunes the bunkers are carved into are now shaped like a wave crashing over the sand. RCD plays to the backdrop of the Mourne Mountains, Ireland's most rugged range and a perfect setting for such a scraggy layout.

My other Northern Ireland favorite lies along the North Atlantic. Royal Portrush is the only course outside of Scotland and England to host the Open Championship. The layout begins its climax on the par-3 sixteenth, aptly named "Calamity Corner." It's 236 yards playing along the edge of a massive sand dune, and I don't know where the Corner aspect comes in, but the Calamity is quite apparent. Nearby Portstewart Golf Club opens with a spectacular nine holes, and almost every green is cradled among sand dunes like baby birds in a nest.

Less-famous courses in smaller towns like Castlerock and Ardglass are classically traditional links, and ancient parkland courses like Royal Belfast Golf Club and Malone Golf Club, or even the modern gem of Lough Erne Resort, are all worth a visit.

An excellent movie called simply *Belfast* documents the Troubles of Northern Ireland. Your troubles will be documented on the scorecard.

NOTES

....
....
....
....

❏ **NO TROUBLES IN NORTHERN IRELAND** Date: ....

ZEAL FOR NEW ZEALAND

I've been to the end of the Earth and damn if there isn't a golf course there. When you arrive at the fifteenth green at Cape Kidnappers Golf Course in Hawke's Bay, New Zealand, you've reached the edge. You can go no further. At the back of the green, the Earth drops straight down several hundred feet to the Pacific Ocean, and there is nothing else to see. Standing on this spot, you take in the as-far-as-the-eye-can-see view and contemplate the enormity of the world and golf's small place in it. Here, where golf, land, and ocean meet so impossibly, you have to wonder how it all got this way.

But then there's the closing stretch at Cape Kidnappers to deal with. The drama of the course—the holes that cling to fingers of land edged by cliffs and canyons so steep and so deep that you couldn't survive if you fell—is behind you. The closing holes are good ones, to be sure, but the whole course can't play at the end of the world, so, luckily, the sixteenth hole turns back toward safer territory.

New Zealand's patchwork history of Māori, European, Pacific Island, and Asian influences makes it a cultural melting pot in a landscape of stunning natural beauty. The world is full of interesting cultures that have an affection for golf, and the land of Kiwi, which is at once a furry fruit, a flightless bird, and a reference to the native population, is certainly one of them. There are more than 400 courses on the two islands, which roughly equate in size to the US East Coast from Boston to Miami. Auckland is about New York City, Wellington is Charleston, South Carolina, and on the South Island, Christchurch is about Orlando. You can travel the entire country and never get farther from the ocean than Atlanta.

The golf from north to south is best described as at times so American you wonder why you flew halfway around the world to play, and at times so spectacular the thought of staying for another week or maybe another decade can't help but enter your mind.

Tara Iti, about 90 miles north of Auckland, the country's cultural center, is craggy ribbons of green fairways that stand out amid sandy waste areas, all cozied up to the great expanse of the Pacific Ocean although much closer to sea level than Cape Kidnappers. The club is private but offers international travelers a one-time option to be treated as a member. That doesn't mean one round of golf. You can visit for a week and play 36 holes a day, but once you leave, you leave for good—unless you become a member.

You can travel the expanse of New Zealand's two islands and find outstanding golf at places like Paraparaumu Beach Golf Club, considered the best links course in the Southern Hemisphere. Other great courses on the North Island include Kinloch Golf Club, Kauri Cliffs Golf Course, where almost every hole has a view of the Pacific, Titirangi Golf Club, Royal Wellington Golf Club, and Royal Auckland and Grange Golf Club. But don't go all the way Down Under without visiting the South Island.

A fellow golf writer describes it this way: "If the North Island is the land of fire and steam (with its volcanoes and thermals), the South Island is certainly the land of water and ice. Ice ages, fault lines, and tectonic plate movements have all made their mark on New Zealand, especially the South Island, which is home to the majestic Southern Alps, a network of fiords and several glaciers that continue to march down into rainforest."

Golf on the North Island is dominated by oceanscape views. The South has mountainscapes, with golf being played beneath snow-peaked ranges at places like Terrace Downs Resort, which is home to some of the most spectacular mountain views from a golf course anywhere in the world. Peppers Clearwater Resort is known for its water features, even though none is the ocean. Jack's Point is often mentioned among New Zealand's most awesome as it sits between The Remarkables mountain range and the cliff tops above Lake Wakatipu. The golf courses may be the most tame places on the South Island. Its rugged topography makes it easy to see why film's cinematic trilogies like *The Lord of the Rings*, *The Hobbit*, and *The Chronicles of Narnia* were all filmed there.

NOTES

. . . .
. . . .
. . . .
. . . .

❏ **ZEAL FOR NEW ZEALAND** Date: . . . .

THE DANGERS OF AUSTRALIA

Long before the first golf ball was struck in Australia and even long before Britain started sending her most hardened criminals to the continent Down Under, Australia was preordained to be a great golf destination thanks to a geologic anomaly that occurred about 20 million years ago. As the earth churned its way toward its current configuration, the retreating ocean left behind a massive vein of sandy loam, at times 250 feet deep, now known as the Melbourne Sand Belt, to the southeast of the city. Now many miles from the sea, it has a geology very similar to the linksland of the British Isles.

Golf came to Australia via the drafting table of Dr. Alister MacKenzie, who would go on to design American classics like Cypress Point, Crystal Downs, and of course, Augusta National. But his first masterpiece was Royal Melbourne Golf Club, where he carved features from the ancient loam that allowed him to cut bunkers right up to the edge of greens for an interesting look that creates a style of play unlike anywhere else in the world. Even after all these years, the course remains one of the world's gems.

While MacKenzie's work at Royal Melbourne is the pinnacle of Australian golf, almost within walking distance of this gem are seven other Sand Belt courses that take advantage of the unusual terrain. Victoria Golf Club is just across Reserve Road from Royal Melbourne and Kingston Heath Golf Club is just a few blocks away. Yarra Yarra Golf Club, Huntingdale Golf Club, Metropolitan Golf Club, and Commonwealth Golf Club occupy land at the crossroads of Centre and Warrigal, just four miles from Royal Melbourne, making this area of Victoria the most condensed neighborhood in the world for world-class golf.

Of course, who's going to travel all the way to Australia to see one neighborhood, as great as that neighborhood might be? Sydney is the point of entry for most tourists and golfers. While the opera house and Harbour Bridge are its dominant features, MacKenzie's design at New South Wales Golf Club is the destination most golfers visiting Sydney care about. It is always ranked among the world's finest. Royal Sydney Golf Club gets good marks as well. Australian media magnate Kerry Packer built a wonderful course in the rugged hills of his Hunter Valley retreat in a very remote part of the state well north of Sydney. While considered a great course, its exclusivity means few have ever gotten to play it.

Australia's most devilish courses, at least in terms of getting to them, are on islands. On Tasmania, Barnbougle Dunes, and Barnbougle Lost Farm are two spectacular courses on the Bass Strait, which separates the island and the Australian mainland. Both play across the incredible dunescape on the north shore of the island with fairways that roll like an angry ocean. It's difficult to get there, but worth it. On the northern point of King Island in the Bass Strait, Cape Wickham has been called the most spectacular course in Australia.

Thankfully, almost all of the great golf Down Under is found in hospitable urban areas. The great Australian Outback and the seas that wash up on the continent's shores are filled with some of the world's deadliest creatures. The great white shark and saltwater crocs, we all know about, but creatures like the inland taipan, the blue-ringed octopus, the textile cone snail, the box jellyfish, and the funnel-web spider can be just as deadly, though not by such gruesome means. Of course, some of the situations you will find yourself in on the golf course are no fun either.

NOTES

. . . .

. . . .

. . . .

❑ **THE DANGERS OF AUSTRALIA** Date: . . . .

GOLF'S OTHER KINGDOM: THAILAND

Bangkok is a city of contrasts. East versus West, old versus new, traditional family lifestyles versus the will to join the developed world. In central Bangkok all of these values collide, most ironically in the fact that 94.6 percent of the population follows the teaching of Buddha but the city nightlife makes Las Vegas look tame. There are dozens of modern high-rise condominiums that help give the city an expansive and modern skyline, but those buildings often cast shadows over traditional street markets that date back hundreds of years and where generations of families have sold local vegetables and herbs that most Westerners wouldn't recognize and have names we can't pronounce. How much *buap hom, fak thong,* or *khilek* do you have on hand?

In contrast to these street markets where sellers are just trying to eke out enough *bhat* to get to the next day are Bangkok golf courses like Nikanti Golf Club, where the luxury and service are over the top. The design is impeccable, the conditions unbelievable, and its layout of three sixes instead of two nines pays tribute to the six realms of

THE GOLF BUCKET LIST

Buddhism. On the other side of the city at a course called Royal Gems Golf City you'll find a bunker-for-bunker replica of the back nine at Augusta. It won't convince you you're in Georgia, but all the elements of each hole are distinctly recognizable.

Of course, you can't visit Thailand without immersing yourself in the famous Thai cuisine, which when spiced up the way the locals eat it packs more heat than Dirty Harry. Your local Thai restaurant just doesn't do the real deal justice. Some of the best Thai food is in small towns and roadside eateries where no English is spoken, so you look at pictures on the menu and point. Almost regardless of where your finger lands a traditional Thai dish arrives at your table, epically delicious and way too much food for what seems like way too little money. But in the end both you and the proprietor are happy.

Golf in these smaller towns is a more earthy experience. At Royal Ratchaburi Golf Club near Kanchanaburi there are no ingenious design elements, but thousands of monkeys roam the fairways freely without regard to your game. They might pack in curiously around your ball in the fairway, but when you get to within a few steps, they will noisily excuse themselves and continue eating bugs from each other's hides somewhere else.

Away from the major cities and resort areas you find the history of Thailand, an ancient country full of palaces and statues of Buddha. For Americans, one of the most fascinating pieces of history is the bridge over the River Kwai. During World War II the Japanese occupied Thailand and planned to advance to Burma but needed a railroad line to move supplies. Allied prisoners and locals were forced to work 18 hours a day building the bridge for the railway that became known as the "railroad of death" because of the incredibly rough terrain, tropical heat, shortage of food, brutality of the Japanese guards, malaria, and poisonous snakes. Near Kanchanaburi, the open-air Jeath War Museum offers a gruesome look at the life of POWs during the occupation. The human toll is contained in two huge cemeteries where more than 9,000 gravestones mark the Allied sacrifice.

At some point on your journey, make time for the famous Thai massage, which I found to fall somewhere between extreme yoga and torture. I was bent and twisted in so many directions that I heretofore didn't know the human body could accommodate that twice I think I started to cry. You will be shocked at the amount of leverage a Thai girl who might not even weigh 100 pounds can exert on the tight and underused muscles of a middle-aged man. And she'll throw more elbows than in most NBA games.

You're sure to stumble upon the equally famous Thai nightlife. Walk down certain streets in many cities and you get the impression that this is a land of reckless abandon when it comes to gaudy nightlife. Bangkok's world-famous Soi Cowboy and Patpong (where parts of *The Deer Hunter* were filmed) cater to international travelers. On the famous Walking Street in the beach town of Pattaya the Hooters restaurant has an almost religious conservatism compared to the overt display of sex on the street. On less-famous but even more lurid Soi 6 in Pattaya, almost every establishment is bathed in pink neon and to walk the street is to walk a gauntlet of what conservative America would call outlandish debauchery.

And then there's the rickshaw. It is still a staple of city travel, but no longer powered by foot. At some point an ingenious rickshawer thought to save himself the tiresome legwork by putting a two-stroke motor on an oversized tricycle with a canopied platform and a bench. The rickshaw is commonly known as a *tuk-tuk* for the sputtering sound the little engine makes. The time will come when you'll need to hail one, but if you think a New York City cab ride is hair raising, it's nothing compared to a death-defying ride on a Thailand tuk-tuk.

. . . .

. . . .

. . . .

. . . .

❑ **GOLF'S OTHER KINGDOM: THAILAND** Date:. . . . .

WHY DUBAI?

The Western world's view of the Middle East is perhaps still skewed by religious conflicts, oil embargos, terrorism, Desert Storm, and the lingering memory of hostages in Iran. And, yes, as a whole, maybe the Middle East could use a good PR agency. And perhaps, it was just that to put Dubai front and center on the world golf stage. A partnership between DP World, a Dubai-based multinational logistics company, and the DP World Tour created the Race to Dubai, the mega-season-ending tournament that annually includes many of the best players in the world.

When these players get to Dubai, they find the antithesis of the general impression of the Middle East. Dubai is an oil-rich emirate that has shared the wealth with its people, creating a society and culture that maintains one of the world's highest standards of living. With that comes golf, but only recently. Oil wasn't discovered in Dubai until the mid-1960s, and the first oil wasn't exported until 1969. Until then the people of the emirate lived a nomadic existence, scraping together a life from the harsh desert living a Bedouin lifestyle. As oil wealth spread, Dubai became a desert oasis of impeccably kept green grass and imported palm trees, a modern city swallowed by a timeless desert. The people live a standard of life not known in many other places in the world, with riches so vast that in 2007, 41 new skyscrapers were built. Dubai, where natives pay no income tax, is now home to the world's tallest building (the 2,717-foot Burg Khalifa), the 3.77-million-square-foot Dubai Mall, and a skyline comparable to New York and Hong Kong.

Modern golf began in 1988 with the opening of Emirates Golf Club, where the now-iconic clubhouse resembles a cluster of Bedouin tents. Built in what was then barren desert miles south of central Dubai, the cityscape of the emirate has grown to reach it and now tee shots play to the backdrop of skyscrapers. Emirates opening is qualified as the first all-grass course in Dubai. The game's history here dates to 1969, when the all-sand Dubai Country Club (DCC) opened. Lines painted in the desert defined fairways, where you could hit off a small artificial-grass mat you carried with you. The other side of the line was considered "rough" and you had to play off the sand rather than the mat. The "greens" were sand mixed with oil and packed tight so putts would roll true but with little break. As modern Dubai expanded, DCC's land became too valuable for sand golf, especially with the proliferation of high-end golf clubs and resorts with green grass. But it survived as an anomaly until 2007.

Dubai Creek Golf and Yacht Club opened in 1993 and hosted the Dubai Desert Classic for many years. The Jebel Ali resort course opened in 1998, and since the turn of the new century, course openings have been a regular occurrence. Resort-style courses like Montgomerie Golf Club Dubai, the Els Club Dubai, Jumeirah Golf Estates, and Dubai Hills Golf Club all play to the backdrop of the modern Dubai skyline.

In other parts of the world you're plagued by the threat of rain hampering your golf trip, but you don't have to worry about that in

Dubai. The average annual rainfall is four inches, yet the courses are ridiculously green, the rough is plush, and the greens are pure, all made possible by an abundance of water from desalination plants. To get a glimpse of what the emirate was like before oil, Heritage Village is to Dubai what Colonial Williamsburg is to the United States. Like Williamsburg, it is a small area devoted to preserving the history of a nation, long before golf ever became a possibility.

NOTES

. . . .
. . . .
. . . .
. . . .

❏ **WHY DUBAI?** Date: . . . .

OH, CANADA

When we think of Canada, sports like ice hockey and alpine skiing come to mind, along with polar bears, the Hudson Bay, and the better side of Niagara Falls. But let's not sell the Great White North short when it comes to golf. Spectacular landscapes often make for spectacular golf, and Canada is short on neither. From high in the Canadian Rockies to the rugged coastal cliffs of Nova Scotia, only the United States, United Kingdom, and Japan surpass Canada in number of golf courses. And when we throw scenery into the mix, we could argue that Canada has a better combination than any. As evidence, play the cliff-hanging seaside holes at Cabot Cliffs Golf

Course in Nova Scotia or the Fairmont Banff Springs Golf Course under the jagged peaks of Alberta.

Any conversation about great Canadian golf courses must begin with Canada's great classic-era course architect Stanley Thompson. He was one of those larger-than-life personas, but he knew what he was doing at the drafting table. He had a hand in more than 160 courses, including Canadian greats like Fairmont Jasper Park Lodge Golf Course, Banff Springs, Royal York/St. George's Golf Club, Capilano Golf and Country Club, and Cape Breton Highlands Links. His two greatest, Jasper Park and Banff Springs, are in the great Canadian Rockies, and each plays beneath a multitude of jagged peaks. Both built before modern equipment was available, they required hundreds of laborers doing a year of back-breaking work clearing land and removing boulders.

The work wasn't quite as difficult in the Canadian maritime provinces and the result wasn't quite as spectacular. Some call Prince Edward Island the capital of Canadian golf, although that's probably more for its bounty of courses. The Links at Crowbush Cove is the golf gem in a land known for lobsters, muscles, and Lucy Maud Montgomery's fictional character Anne of Green Gables. There is a Green Gables Golf Course near the Green Gables heritage site that pays tribute to the author and the character.

Nova Scotia is home to what many consider the country's best course, Cabot Cliffs Golf Course, where fairways and greens nudge up to the edge of 100-foot cliffs overlooking the Gulf of St. Lawrence. It's sister course, Cabot Links, sits on much safer ocean-level ground and plays much like the great links of the British Isles. In the sparsely populated north of Cape Breton Island, the touristy city of Ingonish Beach, where fewer than 3,000 people live, is home to Cape Breton Highlands Links, another highly ranked Canadian course.

Like the United States, Canada's great cities are full of great golf, and also like the United States, much of it is private. Some of the best public courses are in out-of-the-way tourist places like Merrit (Sagebrush Golf Club), Panorama (Greywolf Golf Course), and Vernon (Predator Ridge Resort), all in British Columbia; Gravenhurst (Muskoka Golf Club) and MacTier (Rocky Crest Golf Resort), both in Ontario; Deer Lake (Humber River Golf Club) in Newfoundland, and Canmore (Stewart Creek Golf and Country Club) in Alberta. All of them are worth the trek, however long and difficult it might be.

NOTES

. . . .

. . . .

. . . .

. . . .

❑ **OH, CANADA** Date:. . . . .

CHAPTER 6

10 Books (Besides This One) You Should Read

THE LEGEND OF BAGGER VANCE

It's not often golf collides with scripture. But Stephen Pressfield's golf tale of the metaphysical character of Bagger Vance is loosely based on Bhagavad Gita, a 700-verse Hindu scripture that is part of the Mahabharata, one of two major Sanskrit epics of ancient India. The Mahabharata is the story of the Kurukshetra War between the families of Kauravas and Pāṇḍavas. The central figure is Arjuna, a key warrior of the Pāṇḍava family who deeply considers not fighting because of the harm war will bring to his people. Arjuna seeks the advice of Krishna, a major deity in Hinduism, and the discourse between the two constitutes the Bhagavad Gita.

I have not read the Mahabharata, roughly 1.8 million words, and probably won't tackle it. I have read *The Legend of Bagger Vance* and the central figures are Randolph Junah (R. Junah or Arjuna) and his mystical caddie Bagger Vance (Bhagavad). Set during the Great Depression, Junah, a one-time great amateur player who struggles with what we would identify today as post-traumatic stress disorder following the realities he faced fighting in Europe during WWI. Junah is invited but initially refuses to play in a golf match against Bobby Jones and Walter Hagen, a match concocted to bring publicity to and ultimately save a Savannah, Georgia, golf resort planned, built, and opened just before the stock market crashed, leaving almost no one able to afford the luxury of the Krewe Island resort. Bagger Vance appears through the mist one night, and though Junah doesn't seek his counsel, the two end up in a mentor-mentee relationship as Bagger coaxes Junah to play and then as his caddie guides him through the 36-hole match with some life lessons and observations along the way, just as Krishna gives Arjuna the supreme knowledge of the Bhagavad Gita, which helps him overcome his moral dilemmas.

Pressfield has an interesting story himself. A graduate of Duke University, he served as an infantryman in the US Marine Corps, but after being discharged, he struggled to make ends meet and at one point lived in a nearly condemned house without power, running water, or glass in the windowpanes. He says he picked fruit, drove an 18-wheeler, worked on off-shore oil rigs, and wrote advertising copy before he found his voice with the metaphysical character of Bagger Vance. We appreciate his stick-to-itiveness and would venture to say that the vast library of golf literature would be intellectually depleted without Pressfield's contribution, even if it would be just one book lighter.

NOTES

....

....

....

....

❏ **THE LEGEND OF BAGGER VANCE** Date:........................

FINAL ROUNDS

Golf literature is filled with stories of fathers passing the game on to their sons, and the game becoming their lifelong tie, a connection that lives despite miles that may separate them or troubles that may befall them. I've added my share to decades of such literature, writing about both my father and my son. But on this topic, never have I or any other writer exceeded the work of James Dodson in *Final Rounds*.

Dodson's book is the pinnacle of chronicling how the game often helps define, or at least outline, the father-son relationship in a positive way, even though we know the father-son relationship isn't always positive. Whether chronicled or not, the game has a way of binding fathers and sons. *Final Rounds* is a heartfelt story of a son who takes his terminally ill father on the golf trip of a lifetime through England and Scotland. Dodson uses the trip as the vehicle to tell the story of a father's love for his son and the son's gratitude for his father's genial guidance and always-there-for-you parental philosophy. When Braxton Dodson falls ill, but before he is disabled by the disease, James arranges the trip. The sacred courses, their golf lore, the towns they are in, and the miles driven between become the narrative of the book. But it is the personal reflections and realizations that make the book special. Some writers would find it difficult to reveal such personal details so publicly, but Dodson does so with an easy grace and sophisticated elegance.

Final Rounds is alternately heartwarming and heartbreaking. The reader is fully aware that the trajectory of the book leads to a sad ending, but Dodson refuses to let the writing get bogged down in that. Instead, *Final Rounds* is a tribute to a man who didn't live long enough to appreciate his son's tribute, but it is more a celebration of life and the ultimate way for a son to say thank you, even if it had to be posthumously.

NOTES

. . . .
. . . .
. . . .
. . . .

❏ **FINAL ROUNDS** Date: . . . .

MISSING LINKS

Rick Reilly was *the* sportswriter of my generation, penning columns on the back page of *Sports Illustrated,* which for more than a decade was the reason to subscribe. He wrote on all sports and only occasionally golf, but his first golf-specific book, *Missing Links,* hits home with almost everyone who has ever played the game as a tribute to golf's have-nots.

A group of Boston buddies obsessed with golf but only privy to the local public municipal course (Ponkaquogue Municipal Golf Links and Deli) bet among them to see who can be the first to finagle their way onto the old-money, blueblood country club next door to their beloved-but-tattered muni, which they claim is the single worst golf course in the country. Meanwhile, neighboring Mayflower Country Club beckons with its manicured conditions, smooth and speedy greens, and uncrowded fairways, where only what they view as pompous and pretentious members tread. Among the friends, begging, groveling, lying, and cheating are not only necessary but encouraged as they reach for Boston golf's Holy Grail.

One eventually makes their way on to Mayflower, but it's the laugh-out-loud adventures of Two Down, Dannie, and Stick, along with other characters of the muni during their rounds at the course they call "Ponky," where the truths of their friendships and golf games are revealed, that provide the most hilarious moments of the book. Reilly follows *Missing Links* with *Who's Your Caddy?,* in which he chronicles his inept caddying efforts for pros, high-rolling hustlers, and even a blind golfer, and *Shanks for Nothing,* the sequel to *Missing Links,* with more misadventures at Ponky.

. . . .

. . . .

. . . .

. . . .

❏ **MISSING LINKS** Date:. . . . .

A COURSE CALLED IRELAND, SCOTLAND, AMERICA

Tom Coyne had an idea. The problem was that almost every golf writer, traveling golfer, or perhaps, every golfer period has had the same idea—spend a summer in Ireland playing every course you possibly can. But by the early twenty-first century, almost everything that could be written about Irish golf had been written. So, he came up with a hook. He would walk between the towns along the perimeter of the island of Ireland, where the great and hidden gem courses reside among the dunes. The trip became *A Course Called Ireland: A Long Walk in Search of a Country, a Pint, and the Next Tee.*

Coyne walked the rugged coastline of Ireland, playing every course he came upon—from little Kilkee Golf Club in County Clare to the giant of Ballybunion in County Kerry. His descriptions of the courses he played are almost poetic, but it's the encounters with Irish folks in the small coastal towns that give life to the text. If you haven't been to Ireland, you might not understand how the network of these small towns strung together is the real Ireland. You can go to the country's major resorts but you'll meet mainly other Americans. It's towns like Lahinch, Enniscrone, Ballyliffin, Portrush, Newcastle, Baltray, and on and on where Coyne captures the spirit of Ireland and Irish golf.

As wet, windy, and physically gruesome as his 2007 summer walk was, it served as a springboard to two more volumes. In *A Course Called Scotland: Searching the Home of Golf for the Secret to Its Game,* he plays more than 100 of the oldest and most legendary courses in the world in search of insights to the game's beginning and traditions. Then in *A Course Called America: Fifty States, Five Thousand Fairways, and the Search for the Great American Golf Course,* he visits all 50 states in search of a better understanding of his home country and its residents. In 2025 Coyne plans to release *A Course Called Home.*

NOTES

. . . .

. . . .

. . . .

. . . .

❑ **A COURSE CALLED IRELAND, SCOTLAND, AMERICA**

Date:. . . . .

CLASSIC GOLF STORIES

If we were to rid ourselves of the professional game of golf with its private jets, mega purses, and the spoils that go to the rich and famous; if we were to discount that level of golf and return to the game as it was a century and more ago, one common denominator would be the average player's love for the game. These days we seem consumed by reading about golf's one-percenters, the players that have achieved such a high level of competence that we relate to them not as fellow players but as celebrities.

If we were to strip that away, and all the ink and trees killed to create pages in magazines and books about these few, we would be left with writings equivalent to golf's classic era when not so much of the game's oxygen was soaked up by so few. In a time when professional golfers were essentially second-class in the train that was golf, writing focused on the agony and the ecstasy of the everyday player and that person's joy and frustration with golf.

Classic Golf Stories, edited by Jeff Silverman, homes in on the emotions of golf. The game has tickled the fancy of many a great writer and lends itself to introspective prose more than any other sport. P. G. Wodehouse, F. Scott Fitzgerald, Ring Lardner, Bernard Darwin, and A. A. Milne are among the authors from whom Silverman compiled essays and stories. These great chroniclers and others look inside the game, inside themselves, revealing golf's great joy and utter despair.

NOTES

. . . .
. . . .
. . . .
. . . .

❑ **CLASSIC GOLF STORIES** Date: . . . .

A SEASON IN DORNOCH

On the last night of my only trip to Dornoch my friends and I made an alcohol-infused promise to return. It has gone unfulfilled for 20 years now. In the meantime, Lorne Rubenstein's *A Season in Dornoch* always has filled the vacancy for me.

Were it not for its fabulous course, which I considered to be among the three or four best I've ever played, Dornoch would be just another Scottish seaside village. Without golf, Dornoch would continue on in obscurity like dozens of other Scottish seaside towns that may have a golf course but don't have one anything like Royal Dornoch. The town is special because of golf, but few golf aficionados make the effort to get to the Scottish Highlands.

While Rubenstein's mission was to let golf clear his mind and revive his soul, he found his season turned out to be far more than an introspective golf journey. He gives the reader a feel for more than the town's great course. He brings the place to life through his interaction with locals and shows us that while golf may be the thread that sews the place together, it is the people that breathe life into it. Golfers who come to Dornoch come to play the course. And then they leave. Rubenstein stayed and learned about himself.

NOTES

. . . .

. . . .

. . . .

. . . .

❏ **A SEASON IN DORNOCH** Date: . . . .

GOLF IN THE KINGDOM

Who among us has not at some point observed some metaphysical connection between the game and the spirit? In *Golf in the Kingdom,* Michael Murphy is on his way to India to spend time with the Sri Aurobindo Ashram spiritual community when he makes a stop in Scotland, where he plays a round of golf on the famous-but-fictional Burningbush Links. There, he meets the mysterious golf pro Shivas Irons, who teaches him about golf, spirituality, and that metaphysical connection.

In a mere 24 hours, Murphy's life is transformed. He and Irons play a magical round in which extraordinary things happen. Then, in the midst of a whiskey-infused night, the two take a second crack at the thirteenth, where we meet another mystical figure, Seamus MacDuff. The philosophical aspect of *Golf in the Kingdom* entertains the idea the human soul is far more capable than what humanity has so far attained and that somehow golf can tap into that potential.

Golf in the Kingdom, unlike perhaps any other sports book, lingers through the golfing society still today, more than 50 years after first being published. It spawned the Shivas Irons Society, a group dedicated to the personal growth opportunities entwined in the game of golf. The group believes *Golf in the Kingdom* is "a gospel of those who suspect, or know, that golf is more than a mere pastime." The society claims Murphy's work is about the deeper meanings of the game. I am one to believe that while golf certainly teaches its lessons, those lessons don't extend to the spiritual realm or mystical level. Your opinion may be different.

· ·

· ·

· ·

· ·

❑ **GOLF IN THE KINGDOM** Date:. . . . .

FOLLOWING THROUGH

Perhaps the best golf writer ever, Herbert Warren Wind chronicled the game for nearly half a century writing for *The New Yorker* and *Sports Illustrated*. His thoughtful, eloquent, and insightful essays brought the game to fans in an era before television and digital platforms. *Following Through* is a collection of his best essays that capture some of the most important moments in golf.

Wind's work stands on its own as a road map through golf in the years he was writing, but it is his use of the phrase "Amen Corner" in a *Sports Illustrated* article in 1958 that he is best remembered for. Writing that "history has a way of affixing itself" to the holes in the far-reaching corner of Augusta National, which are annually key to the outcome of the Masters tournament. It's no coincidence that history has a way of affixing itself to great writing as well, and to this day every golfer with any interest in golf's major tournament knows the exact location and make-up of famous Amen Corner, the treacherous eleventh, twelfth, and thirteenth holes where the course makes a sharp turn back toward the clubhouse.

Wind's keen observations of the game, its settings, and the people who play it are poetic and entertaining. Some of his writing is now close to 75 years old, so for modern golfers it can be both a lesson in history and great writing.

NOTES

. . . .

. . . .

. . . .

. . . .

❏ **FOLLOWING THROUGH** Date:. . . . .

DOWN THE FAIRWAY

As Robert Tyre "Bobby" Jones, Jr., points out in the beginning of the classic book *Down the Fairway*, one should probably be older than 25 when writing an autobiography. And had he known what was to come, he certainly would have waited until after his Grand Slam year of 1930, a feat no other player has ever accomplished.

Jones had just become the first player to win both the US and British Open championships in the same year, so he likely figured his career had peaked. So, it seemed a good time to tell his story. *Down the Fairway* was published in 1927, and as with anything Jones touched in those days, it turned to gold. It is now viewed without argument as a classic in golf literature, and it stands as a firsthand account of the golf history Jones created.

The book is a candid and often humorous account of the life of probably the greatest golfer to ever live. Jones's companion in writing the book was O. B. Keeler, a legendary Atlanta sportswriter from the era of old-time newspapering. Keeler traveled with Jones and reported on every significant tournament he won. He is the only person to be present for all 13 of Jones's major victories. Every golfer knows the legend of Bobby Jones, and *Down the Fairway* is his personal account.

In an age of rich and spoiled tournament golfers, Jones's account of his life as an amateur is a refreshing inside look at the most accomplished player of all time.

NOTES

. . . .

. . . .

. . . .

. . . .

❏ **DOWN THE FAIRWAY** Date: . . . .

BLASTED HEATHS AND BLESSED GREENS

Golfers, whether they fulfill the dream or not, all see the game's ancestral home of Scotland as the Holy Grail of the golf trip. To nervously hit the first tee shot at St. Andrews, to trace the footsteps of Ben Hogan at Carnoustie, to successfully avoid the bunkers protecting the Postage Stamp green at Royal Troon. All serious golfers dream of playing on the ancient and famous Scottish links.

In the days before the internet took over with its relentless detail, the golf tourist and dreamer were guided by James W. Finegan's passionate and insightful musings about the courses of the Old Sod in *Blasted Heaths and Blessed Greens, A Golfer's Pilgrimage to the Courses of Scotland*. Finegan was an excellent golfer, and he combines a player's eye with a writer's analysis and a historian's knowledge. His writings on 60 of Scotland's more than 470 courses cover the country's best and oldest links, but he also takes time to account for some of its hidden gems.

Finegan's insights on Scottish courses were collected over 21 trips to the wee country, beginning in 1952 when the aircraft carrier he was serving on anchored in the Firth of Clyde on the west coast of Scotland. During a round with Finegan at his home club of Pine Valley in 1999 (I still have the signed copy of his book that he gave me during post-round libations in the clubhouse), he told me the story of how he and a buddy made their way from the ship to St. Andrews, where they paid 25 pence to play the Old Course. Many of his trips were in a time when travel was not so easy as it is today but playing the great Scottish courses was considerably easier on the bank account.

He follows the book with similar guides of Ireland and England/Wales. The trilogy is a personal accomplishment for Finegan, and his trek through the British Isles is one that all of us envy.

NOTES

. . . .

. . . .

. . . .

. . . .

❏ **BLASTED HEATHS AND BLESSED GREENS** Date:. . . . .

CHAPTER 7

10 International Courses You Need to Play

WHERE IT ALL BEGAN: ST. ANDREWS

The Old Course at St. Andrews is golf's Mt. Everest, even though it sits but a few feet above sea level. In all honesty, the Old Course won't be the greatest links course of your Scottish trip, and if the history of the place could be separated from the present, the Old Course might be just another small-town Scottish links that no one knows much about. It is flat and visually unspectacular, and unlike other great links, is not a course you drive up to and say, "Wow, this is going to be awesome." But when you're immersed in the history and are hitting the shots you've seen many times on television, it will be the greatest golf experience of your life.

First-timers don't always pick up on the subtleties of the Old Course or recognize the strategic planning it requires. You must plot your way around, determining where you want your shot to finish among all the bunkers, many of which you can't see, and then puzzle out the conditions and calculate how to get your ball into the optimal position. Just hitting away is an inadvisable strategy at the Old Course.

Also, unlike other great links, the Old Course has no spectacular holes along the sea. The New Course was wedged between it and the Firth of Clyde in 1895. The New Course is a fine links, though no longer new, and worth playing. While the Old Course is the bucket-list experience, don't go all the way to St. Andrews without playing some of the lesser-known courses in small towns nearby. At the Old Course you're more likely to meet an attorney from San Francisco or a Wall Street investment banker. At places like Crail, Elie Golf House Club, Lunden Links, and Leven, you'll meet the local restauranteur or shopkeeper, and you'll get the true feel of Scottish golf. The Crail Golfing Society is the sixth-oldest golf club in the world. Lundin Links and Leven sit side by side on the Firth of Clyde and once played as a singular course until a rift divided the membership and the course and each faction added nine holes to create its own course. Elie has 16 par 4s and two par 3s. Very cool.

The town of St. Andrews is known as the Auld Grey Toon, but its centuries-old stone buildings and often overcast sky only create that appearance. It's a university town and during the school year it's a lively city scene of fine restaurants, luxury hotels, lively bars, and a well-educated citizenry.

NOTES

. . . .

. . . .

. . . .

. . . .

❏ **WHERE IT ALL BEGAN: ST. ANDREWS** Date:. . . . .

BEAUTY AND THE BEAST: ROYAL COUNTY DOWN

The Victorian period of the United Kingdom saw significant scientific and technological advancements, but it was the brute force of the railroad that cleared the way for what has become perhaps the world's greatest links course and my personal favorite. The Belfast and County Down line reached the little seaside town of Newcastle sometime around 1870, opening it up to summer vacationers who would eventually tote golf clubs.

Club legend has it that a schoolteacher named George Baillie took charge of creating a nine-hole course beneath the Mourne Mountains and on a modest cliff overlooking the Irish Sea. It was immediately popular, so the club parsimoniously commissioned the greatest golfer of the time, Old Tom Morris, to come from St. Andrews to fix what was there and add nine more holes. The club's council said his fee could not exceed £4, which certainly makes Royal County Down golf history's biggest bang for the pound. In the 1920s, Harry Colt adjusted Morris's work and created the links we know today.

The first nine hugs the coast so tightly you can taste the salt air. It may be the best nine holes you ever play. It could also be the hardest. RCD is probably the most natural links of the British Isles, with bunkers so well-worn into place that the scruffy marram and heather on their faces appears to be tumbling down into the sand like a wave breaking in the ocean. On one of my trips here an errant shot on the third hole rolled under the wave. The recovery attempt was the most interesting and confoundedly difficult shot I have ever attempted. But then RCD is full of interesting shots, including the shot to the fourth green that is so blind it requires a 10-foot striped directional pole planted at the top of the dune behind the green. Some say it's quirky. I say it's the best surviving representation of what golf was like more than a century ago.

Over the years, Northern Ireland has had its troubles, but there are plenty of great tourist attractions worth a visit. Giant's Causeway, a 50-million-year-old rock formation along the northern coast near Portrush is the country's most popular attraction for non-golfers. Just south is the town of Bushmills, home to the oldest licensed whiskey distillery in the world. A tour and tasting at the Bushmills distillery is a must. Northern Ireland is the smallest kingdom of the United Kingdom so you can cover a lot of ground. With the exception of Lough Erne, an inland parkland resort course, the great golf of Northern Ireland is along the coast, so pick your way along from

Newcastle to Ardglass Golf Club, Ballycastle Golf Club, Portstewart Golf Club, Castlerock Golf Club, and Portrush, the only Northern Ireland course to host the Open Championship.

NOTES

. . . .

. . . .

. . . .

. . . .

❏ BEAUTY AND THE BEAST: ROYAL COUNTY DOWN

Date: . . . .

SNARLING WITH THE TEETH OF THE DOG

Had the initial idea played out according to plan, the oddly named but eminently gorgeous Caribbean golf course at Casa de Campo called Teeth of the Dog Golf Course would have nowhere near the bite it has now. As the story goes, Alvaro Carta fled communist Cuba and ended up in the Dominican Republic in the late 1960s, operating the financially troubled South Puerto Rico Sugar Company. With financial backing of the huge Gulf and Western empire he built the Sugar Mill in impoverished La Romana into the largest producing mill in the world.

Carta then set out to find investment opportunities in the Dominican. Figuring a tourism industry could draw well-to-do Americans wanting to escape winter, he planned a luxury resort near Santa Domingo. One of the things that would attract tourists, Carta reasoned, would be a golf course. So, he hired fledgling designer Pete Dye to draw up plans for a parkland course on a non-descript piece of land. But when Dye finished, he wondered if there might not be a better place to build a course. Carta said there might be some land near La Romano that was unsuitable for growing sugar cane or grazing livestock. The two checked it out and decided it would be a good place for an executive course for use by employees of the mill. But the more Dye roamed the land adjacent to the Caribbean Sea, the more he visualized golf holes that would be too good for a small course.

Aspects or Assets of Golf

Course rating: A two-digit number followed by one decimal point that is assigned to a course based on its difficulty for an "expert" player, which is defined as a scratch or 0 handicap player.

Handicap: A mathematical calculation of a player's potential ability.

Handicap index: The number to one decimal place that represents a player's scoring potential at different courses based on the difficulty of each course.

Nassau: A golf bet that is actually three bets, one on the front nine, one on the back nine, and one on the overall 18-hole round.

Pin: The flagstick that marks the location of the hole on the green.

Sleeve: A long, narrow box that contains three golf balls.

Scratch: An "expert" golfer with a handicap of 0.

Slope rating: A two- or three-digit number up to a maximum of 155 that indicates the difficulty of a course for a "bogey" golfer, or someone who shoots around 90. Slope and course rating are factored into a player's handicap to determine how many strokes that player should be given at that particular course.

Over the course of the next year, Dye and a sizable local workforce shaped the course, largely by hand, using machetes to clear the stubborn tropical underbrush and sledgehammers, pickaxes, and chisels to chip away at the coral rock. Modern equipment was too costly to import, so topsoil was dragged in cart by cart behind teams of oxen from a mile inland. Dye knew he had the name for the course when he heard crew members refer to the sharp coral rock as "diente del perro" (teeth of the dog), after the canine-teeth appearance of the sharp rock edges. So now, decades later, Casa de Campo guests may think the name refers to the difficulty of the course, but the reality is it refers to the difficulty of building the course.

Now more than half a century old, and much more in dog years, Teeth of the Dog is still drawing tourists and gnawing on their golf games. But with the beauty of the location, the 80-degree weather when it's 30 degrees back home, and the aqua blue of the bathwater-warm Caribbean, you don't mind if the golf course snaps at you.

NOTES

. . . .
. . . .
. . . .
. . . .

❏ **SNARLING WITH THE TEETH OF THE DOG** Date: . . . .

ELEGANCE AND GRACE: ROYAL DORNOCH

I don't remember when it was in the hierarchy of trips to Scotland that my traveling buddies and I finally made the decision to drive north to Dornoch, but it was one of the great golf travel decisions of my life. For years we had read the glowing magazine articles and been wowed by the accompanying images. It looked spectacular, and there is absolutely no reason not to go—except it is a long way north. Dornoch is just 600 miles south of the Arctic Circle, and if you followed the Dornoch's latitude line across to North America, you would have a better chance of running into a polar bear before a person. But you can't say you've played all the great courses of Scotland unless you've made the trip.

It's only a four-hour drive from St. Andrews, but when you try to carve out the time to get there, play, and get back from a week-long trip, it's tough to justify the time—until you actually do it. Then it's time well spent. For most courses, the sun-lit images we see in magazines oversell the course. With Dornoch, they don't do it justice. Up here on the Dornoch Firth, a scenic boundary line of the North Sea, where the summer solstice sun shines for 20 hours, there is no reason not to come. And once you do, it's hard to find a reason to leave.

In the subjectivity of golf course rankings, the links of Royal Dornoch does quite well, but when you get to the third tee and see many of the holes stretched out before you as the course lowers itself to the sea, it's impossible to convince yourself that this isn't the greatest golf spot anywhere. On the right day, at the right time, in the proper sunlight, there is no golf scene to rival it, and I wonder if even Van Gogh could have done it justice.

We walked on, with the constant company of the sea, playing great hole after great hole. The first eight holes played straight out until we were a mile and a half from the clubhouse, and then we turned and played straight home until the seventeenth ushered us back onto the bluff where we started, and then finished, before heading home.

I had finally convinced myself to get there, now I must convince myself to go back.

NOTES

. . . .

. . . .

. . . .

. . . .

❏ **ELEGANCE AND GRACE: ROYAL DORNOCH** Date: . . . .

THE BEST DAY IN GOLF: MUIRFIELD

Some argue that if you're playing golf, it has to be a good day. But there are good days and there are days spent alongside the Honourable Company of Edinburgh Golfers, where the epitome of grace, grandeur, and greatness meet on one of the world's finest courses and inside one of its most stylish clubhouses.

A day at Muirfield Golf Course, where written records of golf date to the 1700s, is simply the best day in golf, not only for the two-rounds-in-a-day format but for the coat-and-tie lunch—we're not talking burgers or hot dogs—as a midday break. Fortunate guests who spend the day at Muirfield will certainly enjoy the sublime greatness of the course that has hosted the Open Championship 16 times. It is said to be the fairest test among Open courses. Though there is no dramatic scenery and no holes are adjacent to the ocean, almost every bunker is a penalty stroke and shots hit offline require difficult recovery shots if they can be found amid the heath and fescues. Nick Faldo once made 18 pars in the final round to win the Open Championship, but to the uninitiated, golf at Muirfield can be brutal. Thankfully, the lunch will be one of the culinary highlights of your life.

It starts with cocktails in the smoking room, followed by a manly feast that pays little regard to calories. A bowl of Cullen skink—an overly thick, creamy traditional Scottish soup of smoked haddock, potatoes, and onions—is always on offer as is the carving of lamb, beef, pork, turkey, and usually a local fish sided by the obligatory Yorkshire pudding, different styles of potatoes, and ample vegetables. And, of course, wine. Plenty of wine. Then dessert. Then perhaps a glass of kümmel, a sweet, clear, caraway-flavored liqueur.

While the jacket and tie requirement (this is in no way optional) between rounds can be a little cumbersome—especially if the day requires tearing on and off raingear—the formality enhances the overall ambiance of a day at venerable Muirfield. On Tuesdays and Thursdays, when visitors are welcome, they share the lunch alongside members on food hall–size tables in a room filled with Muirfield history. Golfers, now lunchers, talk of their morning rounds and anticipation of the afternoon foursomes matches; members alongside guests from all over the world bond over great golf and great food. The membership is so proud of its lunch that they like to say Muirfield is a lunch club that just happens to have a great golf course. So, a day at Muirfield may well tick off both the greatest golf experience of your life and the greatest lunch experience.

. . . .

. . . .

. . . .

. . . .

❏ **THE BEST DAY IN GOLF: MUIRFIELD** Date: . . . .

DOWN UNDER WONDER: ROYAL MELBOURNE

When you go to Royal Melbourne, and you should, don't pronounce it *Mel-born*. It's *Mel-bun*. The Aussies take exception to the rest of the English-speaking world inflicting their style on them. Got that, mate? If only the Aussies could inflict the style of Royal Mel-bun on the rest of the world.

This course is almost always ranked among the world's 10 greatest, and if you're a trophy collector or just an aficionado of classic golf course architecture, this one is a must. The club was forced to relocate from its original Caulfield location in the early 20th century as Melbourne, now a city of five million, grew and suburbia expanded. There is little argument that the work of Alister MacKenzie at the new location became the best course in the Southern Hemisphere. How he did that while spending only nine weeks Down Under and without modern earth-moving equipment is a tribute to his understanding of how golf and nature should live harmoniously on the same piece of land. There is nothing forced about Royal Melbourne.

Here in the Melbourne Sand Belt, where golf and greatness walk hand in hand at several courses, MacKenzie's crafting of large greenside bunkers that chew right into the putting surfaces was a stroke of genius and an artistic look that has never been duplicated. The geological wonder of the ancient Sand Belt makes it a perfect match for golf, and nearby courses like Victoria and Kingston Heath are also world ranked. But Royal Melbourne is the knock-your-socks-off course, and a must-play equal to the best of the British Isles and America.

NOTES

. . . .

. . . .

. . . .

. . . .

❏ **DOWN UNDER WONDER: ROYAL MELBOURNE** Date:. . . . .

KIWI CLIFFHANGER: CAPE KIDNAPPERS

Miss the par-3 sixth at Cape Kidnappers slightly left and you'll be wishing golf hadn't been so hasty in moving away from metal spikes.

When my ball came to rest a few feet to the left of the green here, this meant it was just a few feet to the right of a cliff that plummets several hundred feet down a rocky cliff to the Pacific. A little more traction would have been a good thing.

The wind was blowing so hard toward the ocean that I considered taking an unplayable lie, even though the ball was sitting perfectly fine just a few feet off the fringe. But the angle of the terrain and the unencumbered wind didn't seem like a good combination. I crept to the edge and saw a large grassy ledge 10 feet down, a sort of buffer between golf and death. Relieved that even if I slipped I'd survive, I played the shot and actually saved par.

The sixth is just the first encounter with cliff-side golf at Cape Kidnappers where you might think of the game in Barnum and Bailey terms: death defying. Fairways nudge to the edge of crevasses so steep that if you survived the fall, which you wouldn't, you couldn't possibly climb back up. Greens are pushed to the very edge of available real estate, and the whole setting is so far from any mainstream golf setting that it has to be—almost by definition—one of the world's great courses.

And it is so considered, although it was surpassed in New Zealand greatness by Tari Iti Golf Club, which opened in 2015, and while it is one of many Kiwi courses worth traveling to the two-island nation for, the geographic drama of Cape Kidnappers makes it the one you can't miss. The layout dodges the ocean several times, each time hundreds of feet above the water, which means the views are spectacular but the playing corridors eke out to the edge of livable terrain. Much of the back nine rests on narrow plateaus of land just wide enough for a single hole.

The 6,000-acre resort is a six-hour drive from Auckland, the country's cultural center and embarkation point for most tourists. It then takes 20 minutes to drive from the front gate to the clubhouse on the hairpin turns of Forestry Road. But once you get here you can relax in the understated opulence of the resort. It's quite a ride, both getting here and playing here.

. . . .

. . . .

. . . .

. . . .

❏ **KIWI CLIFFHANGER: CAPE KIDNAPPERS** Date: . . . .

CANADIAN CLAMOR: CABOT CLIFFS

There's something special about an oceanside par 3, but when the hole is so perfectly crafted and placed at exactly the right point in the round, it can elevate a course to greatness. When the hole sits on a bluff 100 feet or so above the Gulf of St. Lawrence, it adds drama to the scene, the shot, and in the case of Cabot Cliffs, the round. The sixteenth requires a tee shot over the jagged cliff holding the hole up out of the water to an area barely big enough for the green for a proper putting surface. It's a hole that can ruin a round or energize you for the closing stretch.

Cabot Cliffs had barely opened before it was considered Canada's top-ranked course and then gradually worked its way into listings of the world's best courses. In fact, take out all the private clubs that only members can play, and Cabot Cliffs moves up into the top 20 or so. The layout at times plays through towering dunes and at times along cliffs that rise more than 100 feet above the Gulf of St. Lawrence in Nova Scotia, one of Canada's maritime provinces. Golf may not be the biggest driver of the local economy (Nova Scotia is the world's largest exporter of Christmas trees, lobster, and gypsum, and it exports more than $1 billion of fish each year), but Cabot Cliffs and its sister course, Cabot Links, are doing their part.

The jaw-dropping scenery of Cape Breton Island, which is the northeast portion of the province, does more than its share to capture visitors' attention, and with half the course exposed to the cliffs the course is named for, Cabot Cliffs makes a sizable contribution. Like many of the newer courses built not for local consumption but to attract traveling golfers, Cabot Cliffs is out there, a three-hour drive from the Halifax airport. But also like many of these newer courses, it's worth it.

NOTES

. . . .
. . . .
. . . .
. . . .

❏ **CANADIAN CLAMOR: CABOT CLIFFS** Date: . . . .

THE BITCH OF BALLYBUNION

The links at Ballybunion to me are at once an object of admiration and a commodity of contempt. I have a love-hate relationship with the old girl. I have made the pilgrimage to Ballybunion a dozen times with a group of friends that has gone there every summer for the last 30 years for the sole purpose of playing the Old Course for six straight days. Why, you ask? So do I.

I have had the honor of scrimmaging with her about 40 times, and she, the honor of kicking my ass 39 of them. There was a round many years ago on a frightfully calm, ridiculously blue-sky day where she did me the pleasure of allowing me a nifty 75, but beyond that epiphany I can't recall a single round across her rugged links where I got the better of her. And I suspect I'll fare about as well in my next 40 go-arounds.

I simply don't have the requisite skills to tackle her mesmerizing charms, her intriguing quirks, her rude unfairness, and quite frankly, her outright bitchiness. I own up to that. If I were to pick the 18 holes from around the world that I've played and dislike the most, six would be at Ballybunion. It's not that they are bad holes, it's just that their over-the-top difficulty is no match for my ability—physical or mental.

I can't tell you how many times I've aimed for the back pin on the ninth green knowing full well that the shot requires such an exacting mid-iron that it is foolish to even try. The smart play is to the front of the green and hope to two-putt, knowing that a three-putt bogey will still be better than most can manage.

The problem with Ballybunion is that your own mistakes compound the calamity the course deals you through no fault of your own. I've played many a quality shot to the sixth green only to have the wind drift it ever so slightly off line and land it a little too close to the roll-away edge of the green, and I watch the shot I had such high hopes for carom into fairway-length swales that surround the green. I've watched many a good player attempt the necessary recovery shot only to face exactly the same shot from the opposite side on their next try.

Sometimes I think the only things missing from Ballybunion are windmills and pirate ships. If Sigmund Freud were to probe the Old Course for sanity, I doubt he would come up with anything more analytical than "bat-shit crazy." I mean, who in his right mind would create a 220-yard, uphill, into-the-wind par 3 over a cavernous and unplayable links wasteland with a small green and barely an inkling of a bail-out area? Or a green with a false front so big and so steep it might be better employed as a skateboard half pipe for Ballybunion youth?

The bitch of Ballybunion often reveals herself like a ghost, and the player who hasn't made an in-depth acquaintance with her may disregard her mordacity the way he would a faint voice or disembodied footsteps in the night. But believe me. If during the course of your round, you hit 10 reasonably good shots that could bounce in your favor, nine-and-a-half of them won't. The bitch.

NOTES

. . . .

. . . .

. . . .

. . . .

❏ **THE BITCH OF BALLYBUNION** Date: . . . .

A ROYAL CONUNDRUM

I don't know of any other course where the dichotomy between the greatness of the links and the monstrosity of the clubhouse is so wide as at Royal Birkdale. To be fair, the inside of the clubhouse is comfortable, elegant, and contains as much "if-these-walls-could-talk" history as any, but it's basically a concrete ship's bridge overlooking the wavy links from which England's greatest course has been carved.

But the course almost never happened. Royal Birkdale dates to 1889, but the club outgrew its original layout, and when the time came to build a new course, it took three years before members could get the support to proceed. Detractors were concerned that golf might be just a passing fad. Thankfully, the last detractors were convinced and the course they came up with, to the links aficionado, is as good or better than most of the courses throughout the United Kingdom and the world. The pure, raw links character oozes from behind every towering dune, and every modification to the course over the last 100 years has kept that in mind.

As for the clubhouse, that has always been a bone of contention at Birkdale. The first one built in 1897 near what is now the fourth green was razed six years later because it was built across the property line. The hastily built replacement lasted only 30 years before the ship's bridge was opened in 1935. But the coolest clubhouse on the property is the original golf professional shop, which stood beside the first clubhouse and is now used by artisan members who trade their skills for free off-hours golf at the club. On the walls are pictures of visitors the little clubhouse has entertained over the years—Nicklaus, Palmer, Watson, Trevino—and now me.

NOTES

. . . .

. . . .

. . . .

. . . .

❏ **A ROYAL CONUNDRUM** Date: . . . .

CHAPTER 8

10 Things You Should Try

HIRING A CADDIE

Relationships, whether they last a lifetime, run the course of, say, a marriage, or maybe dart in and out and survive mostly on resplendent memories, are fragile and fickle, delicate balances of input and out-take and contributions from both sides. Our relationships require an investment of time and energy, thought and effort. You have to call your mother, your father, your kids. You have to hang out with your golf buddies at the nineteenth hole, your church friends at the doughnut table after mass, and your neighbors over yard work, lost pets, or bridge games. You have to think of things to say to hold up your end of the conversation and feign interest in their—as Bruce Springsteen opined—"boring stories of glory days." You have to attend the dreaded block party.

We all could use a relationship on which we can hang a "One Way" sign; a relationship that is thoroughly exploitive, unapologetically selfish, that exists solely for our own benefit. Greedy, you say? Voracious? Damn right. The black-and-white era of the valet ended, and now it's every man for himself—except when you play golf with a caddie. The guy in the white jumpsuit hoists your bag and walks stride for stride with you around every inch of the course, tending to your every need, satisfying your every whim, protecting and nurturing you, fulfilling requests, offering advice, and keeping you from doing stupid things.

A man and his caddie is a beautiful thing—a relationship that needs no tending because it lives, blossoms, and ends in a unique, four-hour environment. It satisfies both partners: you in an egotistical sort of way, him in a fee plus tip. Your caddie, like a valet for a Vanderbilt or Rockefeller in another era, is there to serve you and only you. You toss him the ball, and he wipes it clean. You catch one a little fat and he scrapes the dirt from the grooves. He pops open your umbrella just as it starts to rain and then doesn't try to cop room underneath.

The first time I walked with a real caddie was on my first trip to Scotland. From the huddle of crooked old men in billed tweed caps and a few strapping young bucks gathering around the golf bags just off-loaded from the tour bus, he emerged shouldering my bag. A man and his caddie is a relationship not of choice, but of pure happenstance. Like it or not, this is your relationship.

A big young guy with black curly hair wearing a $600 rain suit covered by a white bib that Woolworth's might have sold for $9.99 emerged from the huddle handling my nylon carry bag as if it were a cozy for toothpicks. He sought me out, stuck out his hand. "Dey cull me Bear. Al'll be oot wit ye tae-dee." And then he went to work. He grabbed a few tees, a scorecard, and a pencil from the starter's table and placed them in the flap of his bib. He reordered my clubs in the bag, making sure numbers followed sequence and that the driver and the putter were in the handiest spots. From across the tee, while another player in the group was preparing to hit, he made eye contact with me then lowered his eyes to the ball in my hand and jutted his chin up to say, "Toss it to me," and I did. He gave it a wipe to make sure I was starting appropriately cleansed. Then, at my turn on the tee, he leaned in and went through a 20-second list of do's and don'ts of the par-five first, as rehearsed as a Shakespearean soliloquy. Then he stepped away, letting go like a mother might send her child off on the first day of school.

In my estimation, a relationship with a sizable guy called Bear could go either way. He could be ornery and grizzly, the kind of guy that in another situation I might not want to meet at all. Turns out, Bear was soft and fluffy and comforting—a grade-school teacher by his Monday to Friday profession—exactly what is called for by a foreigner on the hardscrabble links of the Old Sod.

The caddie is at once an icon and a nonpareil of the game. In the US, we've come to rely on the impersonal golf cart, its on-board global positioning system telling us exactly where we are, exactly where we need to go, and exactly how far it is to get there. The golf cart is order personified—a clip for your scorecard, a holder for your pencil, a place for your beer, a basket for everything else. It's all so calculated. A cart of dispassionate fiberglass and plastic won't put its hand on your shoulder, pull you close and point right down your sightline so you can look down his arm and out over his index finger to the pot bunkers he says you absolutely must avoid, even if it means playing away from the flag. A cart won't tell you that it is "a hunnert and twin-ney fave to coover da greenside boonker," and that the wind is so strong your line has to be the church steeple in the distance well left of where you want your shot to finish. The golf cart can't interpret the situation, read the lay of the land, and mull the elements to come up with exactly the shot you need to play. To the on-board GPS, 151 yards is 151 yards—nothing more, nothing less.

A caddie brings life and adds dimension to the game. He puzzles you out, scrutinizes your swing, gauges your ability, and by the third tee knows that 5-iron is not enough club to reach the 175-yard par 3 because the wind is quartering and it's going to eat up that baby fade you've been hitting. He fixes you, and in return you owe nothing. He shoulders your bag. You walk unencumbered. You have no responsibility other than to make the best swing you can. He takes pride in your work.

Now Bear and I are standing on the 170-yard sixteenth, the breeze is off the back of my left shoulder, and my hand is on the 7-iron. Bear's eyes narrow questioningly, and his face twists and is now contorted in such a way as to say without speaking: Are you sure about that? I move my hand to the 8 and he snatches the bag away, posts it on the edge of the tee, and stands militarily next to it looking down range to the green, refusing to make eye contact and not giving me the opportunity to renege on the selection. I flag it, and Bear is satisfied. "At's a fane sh-yut." He hoists the bag, sticks his hand out to retrieve the club from me, polish it, and put it back in what he has defined as its correct place. He struts confidently to the green to read my birdie putt without so much as an inkling of "I told you so."

No work, few words, two satisfied people. If the best relationships are the simple ones, there is nothing finer than a man and his caddie.

NOTES

. . . .

. . . .

. . . .

. . . .

❏ **HIRING A CADDIE** Date: . . . .

NOT BEING CONSUMED BY THE BET

The pirates at my club are fond of saying of their weekend floggings: "It's not about the money." Of course, they say this as they scrape the day's bounty into their treasure chests. And, like true pirates, they leave no quarter, not even a pitcher of beer into which the pillaged and plundered might cry. A member I call Blackbeard, a 4-handicap swashbuckling around my club as a 10 handicap, is fond of saying he won't get out of bed for anything less than a $20 nassau bet. His mate, Jolly Roger, has told me for years that he'd quit the game if betting were outlawed, thus eliminating his lucrative side hustle. So, clearly it is about the money.

At the casino, the house always wins. In golf there is no house, so the pirates essentially set their own odds, carrying handicap cards more pointed than any cutlass. The bet is a byproduct of a game that is supposedly fair for lesser players to compete against better players via the handicap system. But the handicap system is an honor system, and let's be honest, pirates run roughshod over honor systems.

I guess I still consider myself a purist, not that you can't be a purist and play for money. Certainly, you can, and I do. But to me, the game is still primarily about the inner self and not the greater group. A game of golf well played is an athletic accomplishment, the summoning of physical ability and mental fortitude, and that should be reward itself. You don't need to scrape a pile of Jacksons from the pot to prove your mettle. To me, there is a ruggedness to the game that has been polished over by golf carts, GPS, and fairways that look like they should be vacuumed rather than mowed. Golf was meant to be a battle between you, the course, and the elements. When money becomes more important than the game, we've sold something in our soul.

Occasionally, I have the opportunity to play one of the nearby elite clubs. There are no tee times. The matchmaker sets up the games as members and guests arrive, and usually announces that the club's standard bet of a $2 nassau will be in play. I find it interesting that at an old-money, blueblood club where the net worth probably averages eight figures, the bet is important, but the money is not. When I suggested adopting that as the standard bet at my considerably less-esteemed club, the pirates' haunting and hollow laughter sent chills down my spine.

In my Tuesday morning senior group, we set off before the crowd so we can finish in time to still record some billable hours. We vary the games each time, but if $10 changes hands, it's a lot. The pirates aren't interested in that game. Nothing to plunder. Instead, they arrange games with a little more potential for loot.

"Aye, mateys. We done good today," I often hear one gravelly voiced pirate murmur to the others as they weigh anchor. I don't mind laying a little of my hard-earned treasure on the line, and you shouldn't either, but to be consumed by the money is to belittle the game.

NOTES

. . . .

. . . .

. . . .

. . . .

❏ **NOT BEING CONSUMED BY THE BET** Date:. . . . .

PLAYING A ROUND WITH HICKORY-SHAFTED CLUBS

The box of sand and pail of water on the first tee would have been curious had it not been for the fact that we were standing on the first tee with a bag of hickory clubs and imitation gutta-percha balls. I grabbed a handful of sand, dunked it in the water, and dribbled it into a small pile between the tee markers, then carefully placed my ball on the makeshift tee. This is how it was done before the invention of the wooden (and now plastic) golf tee. I surveyed the wide fairway and figured my best chance to hit it was with a brassie, so I pulled it from the assortment of hickory shafts in the bag. If you've ever wondered why the first fairway on the Old Course at St. Andrews is so wide, you'll find the answer with one swing of an antique hickory-shafted golf club. My particular effort flared off to the right into some scrub grass and I feared I had, with one swing, lost the first of the three balls I got for payment of my green fee. You would think three balls would be plenty to finish nine holes, but then you've never tried to make contact with a whippy tree branch of a golf club.

The most fun part of playing with hickories is using words like mashie or saying, "I think this shot calls for the niblick." Verbally, golf was more colorful in its early days. Back then, you could ask your caddie for the "spoon" or the "jigger" or the "baffy" and he would hand you the appropriate instrument. I pulled clubs from my rented bag of hickories based on how they looked and whether it seemed they might be appropriate for the task at hand. Until this round I never understood why Winston Churchill once called golf "a game whose aim is to hit a very small ball into an even smaller hole with weapons singularly ill-designed for the purpose." Then I hacked my wayward first tee shot out of the scrub grass with a club I was told was a cleek and then used a spoon to advance the ball toward the green, but my poor result necessitated two more swings of these odd-looking tools to finally get the ball on the green. Ill-designed, indeed.

NOTES

. . . .

. . . .

. . . .

. . . .

❑ PLAYING A ROUND WITH HICKORY-SHAFTED CLUBS

Date: . . . .

REVISITING YOUR ROOTS

When my daughter and her family bought a house just a few miles from my childhood home, it was more than a pleasant coincidence. On my first drive to visit her, memories came rushing back as I caught glimpses of my past from the highway. There was the strip of land for the power line transmission towers where the neighborhood kids carved out a rudimentary football and baseball field. And the wooded area that back in the day seemed as big as Sherwood Forest now revealed itself as just some acreage not worthy of development and not really that big at all. The bicycle path we had blazed through the trees to get to the local general store where we would buy fireballs and licorice whips was now overgrown and is indistinguishable, a reflection of societal change that no longer affords kids the opportunity to roam freely.

On my next trip to her new place, I took some backroads, the same backroads where as teens we did things we hoped our parents would never find out about. As I wound my way back to the main highway, I was shocked to find that the driving range where my brothers and I would tag along with my father five decades ago was still there. It was old and decrepit back then, just a half-notch above Roy McAvoy's (the movie *Tin Cup*) driving range, and now, warmly, or perhaps sadly, it hadn't seemed to change. My brothers and I had little interest in golf back then. Our intent was only to hit the car rusting away in the middle of the grass field. While Dad tried to hone his swing for his twice-a-summer outing with other neighborhood dads, we staked out a mat and took turns swiping at striped balls, each of us boasting that this would be the shot that would put another dent in the old jalopy, or perhaps knock it apart once and for all. Of course, we had no chance of hitting a ball that far or that accurately.

Driving by with my clubs in the trunk, I couldn't resist checking it out. And it was everything I'd hoped it would be. The building, a tenement-level shack, had not been upgraded or modernized (or, thankfully, condemned). If the carpet had been changed, it would have been shortly after my last visit, as a worn footpath left no doubt as to how to get to the firing line.

I guessed that the two young girls behind the counter and the cart boy chatting them up were in high school, and I came to the sad realization that their parents possibly weren't even born when I was last here. They handed me a wire basket, kinked and bent and full of balls worn almost dimpleless. I followed the path.

On the line I noticed the upper deck is now closed. We used to beg my father to hit from there so we could get a bird's eye view of the car. I surmised, based on its more-than-slight lean, that the sign forbidding entrance was placed there by a county inspector who had at some point during my decades-long absence deemed it unsafe for human traffic. I found a threadbare mat, hard and unforgiving as the club made contact. I looked up and down the line. The bodies were different but the characters were the same. The old men with 22-handicap swings; the young guys who snuck in some beers and knew nothing about golf but were fixated on hitting the rusty car (the same one?); the couple on a date, although this time it was the girl with the fashioned swing and the boy struggling to hit the ball and wondering what the heck he was doing there.

I've hit balls at dozens of driving ranges like this over the years, but this particular session ran deep with meaning. So little had changed at this range that it wasn't hard to picture my father, now long gone, trying to hit balls while keeping his four sons from walking into someone's 3-iron backswing. But in the ensuing decades, everything has changed since my visit. Dad certainly had no idea that I would take to the game years later and that I would pass the game on to the grandchildren he never met, and now, his great-grandchildren.

Thomas Wolfe told us *You Can't Go Home Again*. But apparently golf can get you there.

NOTES

. . . .

. . . .

. . . .

. . . .

❏ **REVISITING YOUR ROOTS** Date: . . . .

PLAYING A MARATHON DAY OF GOLF

The road of kings may be long and hard, but it's the road of fools that goes one more yard. That's 36 inches I know all too well. One night during a long, cold, golf-less winter a few decades ago, likely a few martinis to the wind, a bunch of us had this idea to play golf from sunup to sundown on the longest day of the year. It seemed like a good idea four months out, so we invited a few friends. And then we decided it should be a competitive tournament. And then we decided that if we hustled we could play 10 rounds in a day. That night we defined the line between genius and insanity—and then crossed it.

Ten rounds of golf under a single bucket of daylight in which you hole every putt, count every stroke, and play every shot down was a bad idea that 92-degree day when we gathered in the parking of a local course sometime in the waning hours of the graveyard shift. Even on the longest day of a Northeastern summer it seemed like an idea that couldn't possibly work. Who's the lamebrain who did the math on this one? Ten rounds, 180 holes equates to five minutes per hole using every available ray of sun. One hole every five minutes. Even with the course cleared of other players for the day, this ain't happenin'.

And it didn't. Damn it, it didn't. Lightning halted the effort at nine rounds, 11 holes. Fifteen of us played that day, from the time you could barely see the ball leaving the clubface until 8:26 p.m. We got tripped up as we headed to the finish line. We did the 26 miles, but we couldn't finish the 385 yards.

The day was brutal: six coats of sunscreen, four coats of bug repellant, three gloves, a dozen Titleists, one 60-degree wedge (crazy stuff happens when you try to play 10 rounds in a day). We had labeled it the golf decathlon, but now it was just a debacalthon.

Yeah, it was a bad idea, but we wanted to see if we could do it so we cranked it up again the next year. Same parking lot, same wee-numbered hour on the clock, same goal. And this time we crossed the finish line. Ten rounds of golf in a single day is still a bad idea. But sometimes bad ideas happen. It was pure agony. In golf, an emergency nine is always fun, and even a second round in the same day is often welcomed. But 10 rounds? That's just insanity.

What's that? You want to do it again next year? Why? We did it. We can't possibly play 11 rounds so what's the point? It was a bad idea the first year; a bad idea the second; and a bad idea the third, but we did it again, and then again the next year. And this bad idea went on for 18 years.

I suppose good things can come from bad ideas, so from this disaster I draw the following: When I'm asked how much golf is too much, I have the answer.

· ·

· ·

· ·

· ·

❏ **PLAYING A MARATHON DAY OF GOLF** Date: ·

FORGETTING ABOUT PAR

Of all the golf history stories that I am tired of, the one about how the term "birdie" was coined at Atlantic City Country Club works on me like consecutive shanks. I don't begrudge ACCC, a wonderful classic golf course. Its claim to fame apparently happened on the twelfth hole, when one member of a foursome stuck a shot to within inches of the cup and another exclaimed that it was a "bird" of a shot. Like many stories before history was meticulously recorded, I accept it and feel no need to challenge it. Although I can't imagine another scenario in which someone would use the word "bird" as an interjection for the exemplary. I mean, did this guy go home that night and tell is wife, "Hon, that was a bird of a meatloaf you made for dinner?"

What grinds my wedge is that there needed to be a term for one-under-par when par itself is such a needless concept. Our compulsion to judge our success every 5.55 percent of the whole leads to 18 opportunities for failure and accompanying angst. Ultimately, golf is no different than other sports in that it's only the score at the end that matters. But because of "par" we agonize over 18 individual micro-games as if each has meaning. What really gets under my skin about par and the terms associated with outcomes above and below it is that it gives everyone a chance to qualify their score over post-round beverages. Ask others in the group what they shot and invariably they answer with their number and then qualify it with how much better it would have been had they not made a triple bogey and two doubles, because, naturally, they were expecting to make par on those holes.

Yes, other sports are segmented. Hockey has three periods, football and basketball, four quarters, and bowling, 10 frames. But the difference is none of them has a required score for each segment. If a baseball team scores no runs in an inning, there is no standard by which that performance is judged, and the game moves on, and all the runs are tallied as they are scored. Bowling gives the player a best-case scenario (strike) and a worst-case scenario (two gutter balls), but makes no judgment as to whether the seven pins you knocked down is good, bad, or indifferent. They're just added to the score that will eventually determine the winner.

Ultimately, that's what golf is, too. Call them all par 3s, call them all par 5s, or call them all par 8s if you want. Who cares? In the end, 71 beats 72; 84 beats 85; 118 beats 119. There is no need to judge ourselves 18 times against an artificial standard to get there.

NOTES

. . . .
. . . .
. . . .
. . . .

❏ **FORGETTING ABOUT PAR** Date:. . . . .

LOWERING YOUR EXPECTATIONS

The other day I got to the range for the Wednesday afternoon game before the pro shop staff had a chance to replenish the striped balls after the morning rush. There were two lonely balls left on a line of what earlier in the day had been a dozen or so neatly piled pyramids. I laced one with my 5-iron and then striped a drive over the 225-yard flag in the air, which for me is quite an accomplishment. I headed out with a smile on my face and optimism in my heart, but no matter how many times this scenario has played out for me, rarely does what occurred on the range mirror what happens on the course. Long ago I decided that golf on the driving range and golf on the course are two entirely different sports, one having about as much relation to the other as football to hopscotch.

I blame the pencil. A four-inch piece of imitation wood and graphite seems an unlikely scapegoat, but once you put that pencil and scorecard in your pocket intending to document your round and measure accomplishment, your mentality changes. Now everything counts. The wide-open spaces of the range and the inside of your head narrow, and the pressure to fulfill the expectations established on the range become real.

A high handicap friend takes lessons and is always practicing. He makes progress but, unfortunately, it's all on the range, where he happily shows off how he's "dropping the club into the slot" rather than casting it from the top as if the range were filled with trout and small-mouth bass. He hits quality shots on the range, but inevitably slap hooks his first drive into the hazard of cattails, reeds, and creepy-crawly creatures on the first hole. His scorecard for the front nine generally looks like a Wendy's order—singles, doubles, triples, and a frosty. So, he punts, says he doesn't care, and then pars the next two holes. Apparently, a little bit of "I don't give a damn" goes a long way in golf. But it's the removal of those expectations that frees him up to swing like he does on the practice tee.

Often, my best rounds are after lengthy periods of not playing. Go a couple of weeks without playing and you show up not expecting much. You go into those rounds without much clutter in the attic. You can't remember that your last round should have been five strokes lower because of bad luck and a couple stupid mistakes. You stand on the first tee with a peaceful, easy feeling, and everything just flows. You're free. You hit some good shots, make a no-brainer putt or two because you're not overthinking the read, and the next thing you know you've carded a good round. So, maybe the way to become a good player is to turn your career into a series of long layoffs.

I tried it one season and my handicap went down a couple points. But the obvious problem eventually emerged: I started expecting to play well in those first rounds back. Those expectations where there weren't supposed to be any expectations soon had me back in my usual spot.

NOTES

. . . .

. . . .

. . . .

. . . .

❑ **LOWERING YOUR EXPECTATIONS** Date: . . . .

NOT BUYING NEW EQUIPMENT EVERY YEAR

A few years ago, I had a pretty good season in club tournaments, so I went to the pro shop on the first late-autumn Saturday that was unfit to play to do a little shopping. I had the assistant pro tabulate my season winnings by going through the tattered cardboard file box he keeps behind the shop counter, where members' certificate winnings accumulate throughout the year in sort of an abacus of a money list.

He announced my total and, apparently, I had an even better year than I thought. So, I wandered around the shop to see what might be useful to my game. I examined the new iron sets racked against the wall, stroked a few putts on the gaudy pro shop carpet, and feigned a few chip shots with some of the new finely grooved wedges still shrink-wrapped in cellophane.

Then I gave kind of a "harumph" of a sigh when I realized I really don't need any of this stuff. From a golf perspective, my life is well-stocked. I'm not a believer that you can buy a game. Plenty of my club mates update their bags annually (or even more often), but I rarely buy new clubs. I stood in the middle of the pro shop pondering the proverbial question that no one ever really expects to face: What do you get a man who has everything?

Golf is generally not a plentiful game, but somehow in mid-life I have accumulated everything I need for the endeavor of not playing to my handicap. Others at my club buy new irons every year, yet they are no better than they were half a dozen sets ago.

I live quite deliberately, and that carries over to my golf life, although you might not agree were you to see how much space my accumulation of golf clutter takes up in the garage. I would say I am wiser than most, or less gullible, in recognizing the marketing promises equipment manufacturers play on the dreams of the average, but in reality, it's just that I'm more of a cheapskate than everyone else.

I recognize that tournament winnings are to be splurged, but my frugality weighs on me, and I just can't bring myself to buy something I don't need, even with play money. Ultimately, it matters not what I walk out of the shop with. It won't change my game or my life. It will just make me feel like I got something for nothing. As I wandered aimlessly in my quest to spend money, the assistant pro noticed the perplexity of my situation and chimed in: "If you don't see what you need, I can order it for you. And we'll match any price." I know this was intended to be helpful, but it only added to my dilemma. With his offer I realized I could get anything I want at a discounted price, so now I can buy more of what I don't need.

NOTES

. . . .
. . . .
. . . .
. . . .

❏ **NOT BUYING NEW EQUIPMENT EVERY YEAR** Date: . . . .

PLAYING A TOUGH COURSE
FROM THE BACK TEE

Godzilla National already had me in a bind. I was on the opening hole, one of the easier ones on a course that claims to go beyond being tougher than nails. Godzilla National is tougher than railroad spikes. So, on the first hole, aptly named Full Nelson, I fluffed my drive and it didn't even reach the fairway. My ball would have been lost in knee-high grass were it not for the hound-dog skills of my caddie. Now I had to try to wedge it up to the fairway and play on. This clearly wasn't the start I was hoping for on what was sure to be the longest round of golf in my life—in more ways than the yardage. But then, that's what I signed up for. I wanted to tackle the hardest course in my area from the back tee, for this single day, to make the game as difficult as possible and see how scarred I would be at the end.

The back tees at Godzilla National card at 7,588 yards, not totally unreasonable these days. But it's in the mountains, three hours up from my house in the piedmont, and many of the shots, like the first tee shot, play uphill. Even in my prime, which, granted, is barely distinguishable from the rest of my career, I wasn't a long hitter. So, my goal was to determine how Joe Average Handicap would fare on a course the USGA rates its difficulty at 79.7 (almost eight strokes over par) and its slope rating for higher handicapped golfers at the maximum of 155, although word around Godzilla's outdoor patio grill is it might approach 185.

The next day, for comparison, I would be playing from the more comfortable member's tee, a good 1,000 yards shorter. Also for comparison, I'd be bringing along some friends: a scratch player, a club professional, and a former PGA Tour pro. And then there would be me, trying to figure out how to manage a monster with my Girl Scout slice that carried 220 yards off the tee when I nutted it. I wasn't sure I'd even be able to finish the course playing by the rules. But first I had to get out of this Full Nelson.

It turned out playing GN from the back tee was like a good high school football team trying to make it to the Super Bowl. You're just going to get hammered. Godzilla National, like many courses built in its vintage of the late 1990s and early 2000s, was intended to be tough. Somehow golf course design got sidetracked and designers, usually at the behest of owners, were told to build a course as long and as hard as possible. As that philosophy turned out, players were willing to give it a try but not so willing to return. Many of these courses are now public parks or pastureland. Those that remain have been softened to more reasonable standards. A few, like Godzilla National, remain gimmicks from the past but are mostly played from three or four tee boxes up from the back.

Somewhere in the haze of the day we got to the middle of the back nine and a hole called Audacity. It was, as Daniel Webster defines, rude and disrespectful. Uphill, 600-some yards with two forced carries over mountain hollows—the second one for me requiring the ill-fated attempt to hit three-wood 200 yards in the air. Another definition of Audacity is the willingness to take bold risks, so laying up was obviously not an option. Usually for me par 5s are appetizers; I can handle them without too much effort. Audacity was breakfast, lunch, and dinner in a single hole.

Finally, we got to 18, a 515-yarder that plays ever so slightly downhill to the clubhouse. Despite the carded length, this is a par 4. It's a bitch of a hole, but it's called Old Bastard. The post-round drinks couldn't come soon enough, and as the first one was served, I tallied the scorecard. The ex-tour pro barely broke 80. Scratch and the club pro barely broke 90. Me? My short drives simply didn't measure up.

I chipped in for par on 17 and holed a no-brainer 40-foot putt on 18 to shoot 94. I'm satisfied.

NOTES

. . . .

. . . .

. . . .

. . . .

❏ PLAYING A TOUGH COURSE FROM THE BACK TEE

Date:. . . . .

EMBRACING TECHNOLOGY

If my father knew I grew up to carry a computer in my briefcase, a phone in my pocket, and a laser in my golf bag, he would think I grew up to be James Bond—or, more likely in my misfit case, Maxwell Smart. Much of the sci-fi gadgetry that allowed the British Secret Service and Control to save the world from the dastardly villains and rogue nations and defeat KAOS are everyday tools we take as much for granted these days as the sand wedge. Many of these tech tools have made their way into golf. These days you can check your email or text your wife with the same device that confirms the yardage to the center of the green and tells you that traffic on the way home is thick, so hang out with your fellas for an extra post-round drink. Maxwell Smart had his shoe phone, we have our smart watches.

I may be a Cold War kid, but I dig technology. It's groovy. The newest gadgets and apps all make my life easier and more enjoyable. When I was banging out term papers on a manual typewriter—often after a late night at the disco in my powder-blue leisure suit—who would have thought that one day I would be able to communicate anywhere in the world with my thumbs while waiting for the pokey foursome in front of me. I remember almost 30 years ago playing a new course because it advertised yardage distances to the center of the green on every sprinkler head. Now that was rad. I couldn't have imagined that I'd outlive such a useful and wonderfully innovative idea. Of course, I wouldn't have imagined I'd outlive the usefulness of the typewriter or (thankfully in this case) the powder-blue leisure suit.

There was a time when the game was played via white 150-yard posts at the edge of every fairway. We eyeballed how far we were from the post and the approximate position of the pin, and drew a club based on that guestimate. It seems very Neanderthal now, and I often think of how the progression of technology has me standing on the tee box on the sixth hole at my club, shooting a laser beam at the pin so it can reflect back to the gizmo in my hand and tell me the distance as well as the distance the shot is actually playing, taking into account the 30-foot drop and the atmospheric pressure and its resistance on a golf ball traveling through it.

For many years I resisted technology in my bag. I fancied myself a purist. I had a wooden club longer than most. While my clubmates were lasering in to the half-yard, I was pacing the distance from the nearest sprinkler head and figuring that was close enough for my ability. While my friends zapped the flagstick for instant results far more accurate than they could possibly need, I wandered the fairway as Moses wandered the desert—knowing exactly what I was looking for but not easily finding it.

I factored in the slope with a wild guess and gauged the wind by the age-old and scientifically proven method of moistening my finger all around and holding it up in the breeze to see which side felt cooler. I computed all of this information—gathered as scientifically as Newton gathered his information about gravity—stepped to my bag, and made a total guess as to which club had the best chance of getting me somewhere in the vicinity of my target, or at least advancing the ball in the required direction.

Our drivers are now bigger and lighter. Our putters are grooved to grasp the ball for a more-pure roll. Our irons are perimeter weighted so it is easier to find the sweet spot. We have digital caddies. But to what end? None of these technological advancements seem to make a difference. Yeah, we know we are 163.5 yards from the pin, and we can now confidently select a club for the task of covering that exact distance, but we still can't hit that club exactingly enough for it to really matter. If all the promises of hitting the ball farther, vectoring in the misses to a more manageable shot-dispersion pattern, rolling the ball on the green more purely, measuring distance via satellites were true, why, as a golfing community, aren't we any better?

Technology has changed not just golf but every facet of our lives. We love our gadgets and could no longer live without our cell phones, our laptops, our laser beams. But has any of it improved us as people? I think not. It's all super cool, but it all just makes it easier to hit our 163.5-yard shot offline.

NOTES

. . . .

. . . .

. . . .

. . . .

❏ **EMBRACING TECHNOLOGY** Date: . . . .

CHAPTER 9

10 Courses You Should Beg, Borrow, or Steal to Play

PINE VALLEY GOLF CLUB

In the days before caller ID, you had to answer the phone. It rang, you picked it up and talked to the person on the other end. It was mandatory. It might be important. Phones of those days had no display to announce the caller, or their digits. No matter how busy you were, no matter how much you didn't want to talk, a ringing phone could be potential business. It could also be a telemarketer pestering you to switch your long-distance carrier and annoyingly interrupting your day's workflow. Reluctantly, I answered.

I was relieved when on the other end was a client who had long ago become a friend even though we lived and worked hundreds of miles apart. Occasionally we shared golf at each other's clubs in each other's town and talked frequently between the times we could meet. He was well connected in the golf world, often working deals between his clients and others that would be inked after a round at his club or the other side's club. On this occasion, he needed to fill a spot in a small group at an away club.

The club was Pine Valley. A couple of weeks later I pulled into the parking lot of the greatest golf course in the world, anticipating a lunch of the club's famous snapper soup and two days of golf in the sandy loam near the great New Jersey Pine Barrens. For all the times I answered the phone and got the telemarketer, this was payback.

Pine Valley has been around since 1918, its combination of history and mystery unique in American golf. It was rarely written about or pictured in the glossy golf magazines other than references to it being the finest golf course in the world. The PGA Tour has never been here and no major tournaments have been held here, so it's sandscape of fairways and greens are never seen on television. The single exception was a 1962 Shell's Wonderful World of Golf match between Gene Littler and Byron Nelson, which you can now see on YouTube. The introduction includes flyover views of a few holes, which give the viewer an idea of how different Pine Valley is. Beyond its annual exclusive invitational called the Crump Cup, the biggest events here are the club championship and member guest tournament. So, the club goes about its business of golf shrouded in secrecy, a haven for members and guests and almost no one else.

The snapper soup did not disappoint. It's heavy, thicker than a bisque. And, as I'm sure you can imagine, the golf didn't disappoint, either. Each hole cuts through thick forestland with fairways and greens lined by large unkempt sandy waste areas full of pleasingly named shrubbery like Crataegus or Scotch broom that may be pleasant to the horticulturist but not the golfer. The course has a look unlike any other and is a test that is among the hardest naturally designed courses in the world. Courses of the make-it-as-hard-as-you-can era of the 1990s and 2000s might play harder but only because of tricked-up design techniques or being built on land not really suitable for golf. Pine Valley is as pure as golf gets, which made my difficult round pure pleasure even though the number in the last box of my scorecard bore little resemblance to my handicap. Dinner in the clubhouse, a night in one of the club's cabins, and a second chance the next day made everything better.

NOTES

. . . .

. . . .

. . . .

. . . .

❑ **PINE VALLEY GOLF CLUB** Date: . . . .

AUGUSTA NATIONAL GOLF CLUB

At some point in my past, likely during some overindulged post-round revelry, I promised myself that the first time I set foot on Augusta National it would be to play the course at the invitation of a green-jacketed member. The obvious problem is I know no one with a green jacket from Augusta National, so my wait continues on in its lengthy futility. At this point it would probably be easier for me to get to Augusta by winning a tournament on the PGA Tour, but that's not going to happen. I lucked into a round on the country's greatest course, so I'll just wait for the phone to ring for the invite to its next-greatest.

I've declined opportunities to attend the Masters because I've never been particularly keen on watching other people play golf, especially since they play a version of the game I can't really wrap my head around. It would never occur to me to try to bend my tee shot right to left on the famous par-5 thirteenth known as Azalea and then loft a hybrid club to the green across the even-more-famous Rae's Creek to get home in two and putt for eagle like they do on TV every April. I'd likely squib my tee shot into the pine straw on the right, play some kind of semi-useful recovery shot back to the fairway, dump my 175-yard approach into Rae's Creek, and make a total mess of one of the most important tournament golf holes in the world.

I'm not saying it wouldn't be an honor and a pleasure to mess up Azalea, but in our minds as we watch the Masters unfold each April we dream about how we would play each hole as perfectly as our ability would allow, as if we would have our best game for the entire round at Augusta. But I'm a realist. I know my round at Augusta would be full of mishits and missed opportunities. I know I'd likely putt a ball or two off the green and embarrass myself chipping back on. So as unlikely as that phone call is to come, I'm content with that.

· ·

· ·

· ·

· ·

❏ **AUGUSTA NATIONAL GOLF CLUB** Date: ·

CYPRESS POINT CLUB

I have a friend who has played Cypress Point. I don't begrudge him that pleasure, but it just shows how democratic the game is. I'm a better player. I get filet from a butcher, not plastic-wrapped hamburger from a grocery store. I enjoy a Burgundy from Gevrey-Chambertin le Clos St. Jacques while he swills Budweiser. But he has been invited to one of the most coveted tee times in the world, and I have not. And he rubs it in by telling me he played well, on a gorgeous day, alongside his father, walking with a caddie among the wonderfully natural setting of cypress trees, dunes, and cliffs overhanging the great Pacific Ocean. I'm jealous. And he's played Pine Valley, too. Now I'm downright aggravated.

I've played Pebble Beach, and that's a notch on anyone's golf bag. But let's be honest, as spectacular as it is, it's a public course that anyone who coughs up enough ducats can play. I've played others along the famous 17-Mile Drive on the Monterey Peninsula, and I've been fortunate to play more than my share of great courses, but Cypress Point rises to the level of unattainability for almost everyone. Every time my friend brings this up—and it's often—I agonize over my mind's-eye picture of him playing the spectacular back-to-back oceanside par 3s, or scouring the pro shop for the cheapest logoed item he can find—a five-and-dime shopper on Park Avenue.

There is no means test for who can play what courses, and that's the great thing about golf. Good fortune can get any golfer to any course, no matter how exclusive. The great designer Alister MacKenzie said of his work at Cypress Point: "The world's greatest artist would find it impossible to tell where nature ended and artificiality commenced." It would be very possible to see where Cypress Point members ended and my friend commenced, but he's been there, and I haven't, and for that I give him his due.

NOTES

. . . .

. . . .

. . . .

. . . .

❏ **CYPRESS POINT CLUB** Date: . . . .

OAKMONT COUNTRY CLUB

Like I said, I've been very fortunate to play courses that most can't and Oakmont Country Club is one of them. As life proves time and again, it's not what you know, it's who you know. And I know this guy who knows this guy who is a member at Oakmont. So, one day this guy calls up my friend, who calls me up, and a couple days later I'm eating lunch in the iconic green, many-gabled clubhouse and having trouble containing my excitement because I know on the other side of the grill room wall is what might be the hardest course in the country, maybe the world. And I'm teeing it up there in less than an hour.

Oakmont has held more US Opens than any other club, and the members like to brag that, unlike all those other US Open sites, the USGA doesn't have to make their course any tougher when the national championship stops by. That's probably not entirely true, but probably less work goes into making Oakmont tournament ready than the others. It is a natural beast of narrow fairways, conniving and plentiful bunkers, firm and ridiculously fast green, and rough that reaches up to the knot in your shoelaces. The club's founder, Henry Clay Fownes, was an excellent player and designed the course himself because he found others in the area too easy. What's impressive about his work is that he had no golf course design experience, and Oakmont, considered a giant of American golf almost since its opening, was the only course he ever drew up. Not bad work for a one-and-done design that has an interstate highway running through it. The Pennsylvania Turnpike bisects the layout. Fownes's original design had members traipsing onto Hulton Road to get from the first green to the second tee and then again from the eighth green to the ninth tee to get across what was then a railroad line. The club built a walking bridge in 1920, and it sufficed until the 1994 US Open when the narrow footbridge created logjams of players, caddies, and spectators. The USGA said it could never bring the national championship back to Oakmont because of this, so with the help of a member who was a Wall Street hedge fund manager, the club built a second, wider bridge. The US Open returned in 2007.

You'd think a course with features like a one-time designer and an interstate running through it would be more of a junky muni. But I can speak from personal experience, it all works at Oakmont—but probably only at Oakmont.

NOTES

. . . .

. . . .

. . . .

. . . .

❏ **OAKMONT COUNTRY CLUB** Date: . . . .

WINGED FOOT GOLF CLUB

One of my daughters went to a fancy private college in New York City, and one day during her freshman year a nicely enveloped invitation addressed to me arrived at the house. It turns out the men's golf coach at her school was invested in helping non-golfer students, especially those in need of financial help, to attend the prestigious university. So, he annually held a golf outing at his country club for just that purpose. So, there it was in my hand, an invitation to play his country club—Winged Foot. And not just golf, but dinner in the historic stone clubhouse, which is listed on the National Register of Historic Places, and probably a peek into the storied locker room. The fabled club near New York City is the work of A. W. Tillinghast, one of the classic era's great course designers, and is always ranked among the best dozen or so courses in the US. And also, as we know, Winged Foot's fairways have been tread by many of the game's greatest players. It has held the US Open championship six times dating back to Bobby Jones's win in 1929.

I thought, "Wow, this is great. The money I'm investing in my daughter's education is already paying off." I read on and was stunned when I came across the significantly steep, and I mean significantly steep, cost for a single to play. My daughter got to this university largely on her academic brilliance, which translated into scholarship money, possibly some of it from this very fund. So, while the figure in the invitation may have looked like a worthy charitable contribution to other parents, to me it was practically a year's worth of dues to my workingman club.

The invitation came each of the next three years, and by the fourth year I didn't even open it; I just set it aside on my desk thinking maybe I'd work up the gumption to open it and actually act on it. But it just collected dust until the day after the outing, when I knew it was safe to throw it away. Now, all these years later, I think I made the wrong decision, maybe not four times but at least once. It's only money, right? But at the time, in the midst of three college educations, that money mattered. So, I passed on likely my only opportunity to play another of the country's greatest courses.

NOTES

. . . .
. . . .
. . . .
. . . .

❑ **WINGED FOOT GOLF CLUB** Date:. . . . .

SHINNECOCK HILLS GOLF CLUB

Embarrassingly, I have begged to play this esteemed club. My son-in-law's family is from a Long Island town near Southampton, where this great links resides on a small pocket of sandy loam shared by the National Golf Links of America and Sebonack Golf Club, between the Atlantic Ocean and the Great Peconic Bay. Nowhere else do three of the US's top 50 courses abut. And the Seth Raynor-designed Southampton Golf Club is a neighbor as well. I would take a tee time at any of them, but Shinnecock is the Holy Grail of Long Island, and I've begged my son-in-law's family to see if they have a connection that would be willing to host me. No luck so far.

At Shinnecock it is the history, the US Open heritage, the resemblance to the great links of the British Isles, and the fact that the clubhouse was built in 1892 and is the oldest in the country. It's all those things a traditionalist like me desires in a golf club. Really? Your family goes back generations in this area where the island splits into a north and south fork, and you don't know anyone who can get me on? I'm begging again, aren't I?

It's just that, of all the great courses from sea to shining sea in this country, Shinnecock is spiritually different, more akin to Royal Birkdale or perhaps Royal Dornoch than to any of its American brethren. There is simply none of this type of linksland left in the US. It's all been developed into beachside homes and condos for vacationers to rent for a week each summer and bask in the warmth of weather appropriate for bathing suits, such weather that is absent in the British Isles. So, the linksland on the other side of the Atlantic remains dedicated to great golf, although those courses are all accessible to me and Shinnecock is not—apparently no matter how much I beg.

NOTES

❑ **SHINNECOCK HILLS GOLF CLUB** Date: ....

7

SEMINOLE GOLF CLUB

I'll be honest, I'm not a huge fan of Florida golf—its flatness, its wind, its arrival of 5 p.m. darkness during the peak season. I am, however, a huge fan of Florida warmth, and sometime between the New Year and the calendric signal that spring has arrived—those days when my course is either a parkland of snowy white, a soupy mixture of grass over mud, or the equivalent of the "Frozen Tundra" of Lambeau Field in Green Bay—I do head to the Sunshine State for a break.

My guess is I would change my mind about Florida golf if I were to receive an invitation to play Seminole. Seminole is one of the exceptions of featureless Florida golf, where small spits of water and large bits of condos are far too prevalent along fairways. Sure, the occasional alligator adds an interesting element, but my course back home has a bald eagle and is occasionally visited by a black bear. Seminole sits on a small trapezoid of 140 acres wedged between Jimmy Buffett's famous Route A1A and the Atlantic, but designer Donald Ross coaxed the best out of the land that was scrubby sand dunes and swampy bottomland. He drained the swamp to create the middle of

the course. He used the oceanside dune for the closing holes, and a bigger dune on the west edge of the property to create several full holes and spots for the tees and greens of other holes.

Seminole opened in 1929, and had Florida golf progressed along its design trajectory, I'm sure I would favor it more. But the rest of Florida's oceanside land developed along a very different path, so Seminole stands as an exclusive enclave to terrain that once was. Seminole's membership at one point included Joseph P. Kennedy, Paul Mellon, Henry Ford II, Jack Chrysler, Robert Vanderbilt, and John Pillsbury. Despite this prominence of members, Seminole legend has it that the membership committee turned down Jack Nicklaus. I'd be curious to hear its reason.

NOTES

· ·

· ·

· ·

· ·

❑ **SEMINOLE GOLF CLUB** Date: ·

MERION GOLF CLUB

Among cities with underrated golf, Philadelphia is number one. Within the city and its suburban orbit lie Pine Valley, Aronimink Golf Club, Philadelphia Cricket Club, Philadelphia Country Club, Huntingdon Valley Country Club, and of course, Merion, a club where history oozes in thickness greater than almost any other. It was here that Bobby Jones first played in a national championship in 1916 as a 14-year-old, here in 1924 when he won the first of his five US Amateur titles, and here in 1930 that he became the only golfer in history to win the game's four major titles—the Grand Slam. The eighteenth fairway was the site of Ben Hogan's famous 1-iron shot in the final round of the 1950 US Open. You've seen the picture of Hogan's follow-through as he watches his shot land on the green to set up a two-putt par and force a playoff, which he won the next day.

The club's roots date to the late nineteenth century, and its historic East Course, to 1912. Its list of national championships held outdoes almost all others. Designer Hugh Wilson wedged Merion into 120 acres in the city's western suburbs, which close in so tight around the course, there isn't an ounce of room for growth. Despite its modest length in today's game, Merion puts up such a fierce battle that in the last US Open held here in 2013, not a single player finished under par.

Its narrow fairways, thick rough, and deep, craggy-edged bunkers all make Merion tougher than Rocky and less delicate than Philly football fans (they once booed Santa Claus). But a tee time here is more coveted than a year of free cheesesteaks at Dalessandro's. But for a golfer like me, Merion is even more tasty.

NOTES

. . . .
. . . .
. . . .
. . . .

❏ **MERION GOLF CLUB** Date: . . . .

LOS ANGELES COUNTRY CLUB

Hollywood legend has it that Groucho Marx's famous line was uttered after the membership committee at Los Angeles Country Club (LACC) denied his application. As if to imply he didn't care, he said: "I don't want to belong to any club that would have me as a member." There is evidence that this story is just another piece of Hollywood legend, but Groucho ended up as a member at Hillcrest Country Club, one of the other tony LA area clubs, but one that caters more to Hollywood types. George Burns, Frank Sinatra, Jack Lemmon, Jack Benny, Sidney Poitier, Danny Kaye, and Milton Berle were all members. Other ritzy LA clubs, like Bel-Air Country Club, Riveria Country Club, Lakeside Golf Club, and Wilshire Country Club, are all celebrity adorned. But LACC is perhaps better known for its list of membership applications rejected—Marx, Bing Crosby, Hugh Hefner, and Randolph Scott at the top of that list. Scott, upon being told he couldn't join due to his celebrity status, issued a Groucho-like line: "I'm not an actor, and I have 50 films to prove it." Although this, too, is likely a bit of tabloid gossip. Another story has Victor Mature being declined and spouting the exact same line but at the time he had "64 films to prove it."

When an LA club isn't interested in celebrities, it must be exclusive. While the asterisk notation on the LACC membership application may say celebrities need not apply, Ronald Reagan did get in, but when he was governor and no longer in films. LACC then granted him an honorary membership when he returned from the White House, and he played regularly there. Maybe it all goes to show that nothing is real in Hollywood, although the LACC course itself is very real. The North Course hosted the 2023 US Open and is ranked among the country's 20 best. Another bit of Hollywood legend has it that members bought most of the tickets to that US Open to limit the general public's foot-tromping damage to their course. So, I wonder just exactly how exclusive LACC is, who is a member there, and how do I get an invite?

NOTES

....
....
....
....

❏ **LOS ANGELES COUNTRY CLUB** Date:.........................

THE COUNTRY CLUB

The legend of The Country Club swirls around the young amateur Francis Ouimet, a caddie at the club who qualified for the 1913 US Open and then took down the game's biggest stars—Ted Ray, Harry Vardon—in a playoff. In an era when the game was only for the wealthy, Ouimet's lineage of a working-class Irish and French-Canadian immigrant family was the stuff movies are made of—and we've all seen *The Greatest Game Ever Played.* And then, of course, there was the game-shattering US comeback victory in the 1999 Ryder Cup, not to mention four US Opens and six US Amateurs held at the club in Brookline, Massachusetts, that is of such exclusivity, its moniker doesn't need a descriptive place name.

The Country Club was the first country club in America to include golf, and the game has now been played there in three different centuries. The legend of membership at the club informally requires that members stay so low-key that their name should only appear in the newspaper twice—once at birth and once at death. Even Tom Brady was denied several times, supposedly because his quarterbacking kept his name in the paper much too frequently. He eventually got it, but the rest of the membership roster is held close to the golf vest. So even moving to Boston and trying to befriend a member would be difficult. The easiest way to get a tee time might be to qualify for the 2038 US Open. As a writer, my name has been in the newspaper way too many times to be considered for membership, but perhaps not enough to be invited as a guest?

NOTES

· ·

· ·

· ·

· ·

❏ **THE COUNTRY CLUB** Date: ·

CHAPTER 10

10 Daring Adventures You Should Try

TACKLE THE WORLD'S LONGEST COURSE: NULLARBOR LINKS

On the Eyre Highway across the Nullarbor Plain in southern Australia, the game comes full circle. What reason other than monotony could there have been for Scottish sheep herders to start knocking a rock around the linksland and into a rabbit hole and counting the strokes it took to do so? Likewise, the monotony of driving across the barren saltbrush-covered desert of southern Australia is the reason Nullarbor Links, the longest golf course in the world, exists.

Nullarbor is 18 holes at various points along the Eyre, a two-lane strip of asphalt so flat and at times so unyieldingly straight that you beg for a geographic feature—something, anything, to break the monotony. But there are no overpasses, no underpasses, no inclines or declines, just monotonous sameness. Until you come upon the next golf hole. From Port Augusta to Norseman, the Eyre, and therefore Nullarbor, covers 1,034 miles with golf to break up the drive. Some holes are on proper golf courses, some on makeshift courses, and some just solo holes built at wayside roadhouses.

With a speed limit of 68 miles per hour (110 kilometers) except in built-up areas—and built-up along much of the highway means places like Eucla (population 53), Nullarbor (71), Kyancutta (79), Iron Knob (199), or the massive Kimba (629)—a through drive would take 15 hours, which is why truckers and travelers stop every 50 or 60 miles to stretch their legs and hone their swings.

You play Nullarbor Links for the experience, not for the score. The rough is often the rocky desert of the Australian outback that is inhospitable for golf but very hospitable to creatures like cute-but-sometimes-vicious kangaroos, Stimson's pythons, and its assortment of fellow venomous snakes, dingoes, wombats, the well-camouflaged thorny devils and Australian feral camels. At least there aren't many crocs along the way.

The golf is the most exotic at the one-hole roadhouse stops where you won't see a blade of real grass. At Nundroo Roadhouse you fuel up and take your swings at the 569-yard Wombat Hole, which doglegs right for no reason at all other than the plow operator who smoothed the Australian outback to create the dirt fairway decided so. Then you might hop back in your vehicle and drive 90 minutes to the Nullarbor Roadhouse, where you play the 588-yard Dingo's Den and maybe spend the night in the basic accommodations of the roadhouse and dine on the local delicacy of King George whiting, an ocean fish endemic to the south coast of Australia.

As with many ideas that straddle the line of genius and insanity, Nullarbor Links was born of an alcohol-fueled night between Eyre highwaymen Alf Caputo and Bob Bongiorno, who schemed over a bottle of red wine for ways to encourage travelers to avoid fatigue and stop and spend money in blink-and-you'll-miss-it places like Cocklebiddy or Mundrabilla or Caiguna. It was in the roadhouse at Balladonia that the two figured golf was the answer. Apparently they were right.

NOTES

. . . .

. . . .

. . . .

. . . .

❏ **PLAY NULLARBOR LINKS** Date:. . . . .

PLAY THE BEST COURSE IN
AN ARCTIC REGION

Once, a player at Lofoten Links in the nether regions of Norway played golf for 30 consecutive hours. Lofoten Links is on the sixty-eighth parallel, which puts it almost 100 miles inside the Arctic Circle, and while there are several courses inside the sixtieth parallel where Santa Claus is more likely to play than you or I, this one stands alone. It's not some gimmick. It's not some little nine-holer carved out to satisfy the golf hunger of the smattering of local residents. Lofoten Links is real-deal, championship-caliber golf in a spectacular setting along the Norwegian Sea unlike any other seaside course in the world. PGA Tour player and Oslo native Viktor Hovland once drove 22 hours to play it.

Lofoten is a long-established Viking settlement that has been inhabited for more than a millennium, but golf has been here only since around the turn of the twenty-first century, when a six-hole course was built. It took another decade to expand it to nine holes, and then a few years later, the existing holes were remodeled and nine more were added to get to the current picturesque configuration. To walk the course, you can't help but wonder how golf came to such a rocky, jagged, and seemingly inhospitable site. But you're glad it did.

At summer's peak, the sun never sets, and late in the short golf season you can play golf by day and catch the aurora borealis by night. But those pleasing scenes don't change the fact that Lofoten may be as tough as the Vikings who developed a fishing industry here. The course is loaded with forced carries and small targets with some fairways and greens nestled into rocky outcrops so close to the playing surface that a shot hit modestly offline might bounce into the Norwegian Sea to swim with the cod.

And, let's face it, a course this remote is not easy to get to. It requires a commuter flight from Oslo and a 45-minute drive. But when you do get here, there is more than just golf. You can kayak with orcas, surf at Unstad or Flakstad beach, climb Svolvaergeita mountain, or hike in the hills or along the beach. But golf is the reason you came, and one round at Lofoten Links just won't suffice.

NOTES

. . . .

. . . .

. . . .

. . . .

❏ **PLAY IN THE ARCTIC REGION** Date: . . . .

SEARCH FOR AFRICA'S BIG FIVE WITH YOUR CLUBS

The lion cubs frolicking not far from the safari bus seem a contrast to the realities of life on the South African savanna. The nearby adult lions, kings of their domain, represent raw power while the tiny cubs define the frailty of new life. The life cycle that will take the little ones to adulthood will be filled with the blood-and-guts destruction of life, a testament to both the majesty and cruelty of the animal kingdom. The fact that I've been here to witness this wonderful and perfectly natural scene is only because humans have ascended to the top of the kingdom, our opposable thumbs having been put to the appropriate use of building the instruments of that ascension—and holding golf clubs.

You travel all the way to South Africa in hopes of catching a glimpse of the big 5 (lion, leopard, rhinoceros, elephant, and African buffalo) on a safari in Kruger National Park, but you also want to tick off at least five of the big golf courses the country offers. And South Africa offers something few other of the major golf destinations can—fine wine. Not bottles imported from other great wine-producing regions of the world but created from the terroir of local vineyards, where wines made from the emerging greatness of the chenin blanc grape dominate lists of the country's best wines. For travelers, their opposable thumbs wrapped around cameras, wine glasses, and golf clubs, we search out the best—the photo of the lions or zebras or rhinoceros, a bottle of Skaliekop from the David and Nadia Vineyard in Swartland, and courses from a smorgasbord of greatness.

Leopard Creek Country Club sits at the edge of Kruger National Park in a bend of the Crocodile River. Spectators likely to spy your foursome include the river's namesake as well as hippos, antelope, buffalo, and elephants. Fancourt Luxury Hotel and Resort, the country's most well-known layout, was the site of the famously tied 2003 President's Cup. The elevation changes at Arabella Golf Course make for spectacular views and challenging shots. South Africa's greatest golfer of all time, Gary Player, has a course named for him at Sun City, the country's most glitzy resort. Durban Country Club sidles up to the Indian Ocean and the fairways undulate almost in cadence with the sea. And you can pick from dozens more South African courses to create your own big five because the depth of the country's selection is great.

But while other golf destinations have their history, their great golf, their whiskey, the bathwater-warm seas, only in South Africa can you get an up-close-and-personal look at some of the most majestic creatures on the planet—and do so from the luxury of a fine hotel or the opulence of a "rugged" base camp. It's an experience unmatched.

NOTES

. . . .

. . . .

. . . .

. . . .

❏ **PLAY AND SAFARI IN AFRICA** Date:. . . . .

PLAY ON SAND GREENS

Every summer my parents would pile their six kids into a wood-paneled Country Squire station wagon for a halfway-across-the-country drive to the small southwestern Minnesota farming town where my mother grew up. Dad would pack his clubs for his annual grudge match with Uncle Ray in a roof rack because we were shoulder to shoulder in the 95-cubic-foot interior that left barely enough elbow room to pick your nose. Not far from my grandmother's house was the town park, and somewhere around my junior high school years what could loosely be described as a golf course appeared near the baseball diamond.

Apparently, some of the area farmers decided to take up the game and plowed some sand greens into what had been a vacant field. In the era of the Country Squire station wagon, parents were perfectly comfortable letting their kids roam free and didn't even start to worry about them until they missed dinner. So, one day my three brothers and I copped a few of Dad's clubs and some of his Arnold Palmer Charger golf balls and wandered across the highway to the "course."

We smacked balls around until somehow they landed on the first "green." Unsure how to putt, we noticed what amounted to an iron T-square lying along the side of the green. We pulled it across the green, and it made a smooth, three-foot wide path on which to putt. The greens were flat, like all of southwest Minnesota, so three feet was plenty to accommodate the half-inch of break any putt might incur. We didn't lose any balls since the course was a wide-open field, and Dad didn't notice his clubs went missing for a day, so we went back the next day. But when we returned the following summer, the course was gone. Apparently, farmers had more important concerns, like perusing the Burpee catalog, considering droughts, and dealing with farm subsidies.

Many decades later, while traveling in the Middle East, I came across another sand course, this one with fairways defined by white lines painted in the sand from which you could hit off a small piece of a driving-range mat issued with your paid "brown" fee. The sand for the greens was mixed with oil to make them soft enough to hold an approach shot but firm enough to roll a putt. The course management did ask you to smooth over your footprints with a broom as you exited the brown. Sadly, this course, too, is gone.

Sand greens were once quite common in this country; even the great Pinehurst No. 2 began with sand greens. Even in this modern era of agronomy, the game played on sand is not extinct. There are a few sand courses left in the Middle East. Some green pastures with sand greens like the one in southwest Minnesota still exist in the remote towns of the Great Plains and up into Saskatchewan, Canada. But these days you need to seek it out—and you should. Like hickory shafts, sand greens are a throw-back to the game's roots in North America.

NOTES

. . . .
. . . .
. . . .
. . . .

❏ **PLAY ON SAND GREENS** Date: . . . .

CONQUER THE EXTREME NINETEENTH HOLE

I don't do helicopters. It's a reaction to once seeing one crashed in a field with three mangled bodies amid the wreckage. I'm also acrophobic. So, hitting this tee shot, the most daring tee shot ever conceived, is not on my bucket list. But if you don't mind choppering up to a tee box that hangs on a cliffside 430 yards above your target, then by all means, put it on yours.

This is the most thrilling gimmick in golf—a short-but-daring helicopter ride up Hanglip mountain to a small driving range mat, from which you can creep to the edge of a cliff and see a massive green shaped like Africa 400 yards in the distance. The extreme drop makes the shot the equivalent of 280 yards, so driver is the only option. You don't risk your life here for a single shot. You get six swings and if you hit a nice, soaring shot, it will take about 40 seconds for the ball to land on the green, or more likely, somewhere in the African outback. The helicopter crew radios the general direction of the shot to a spotter on the ground. If one of your balls is actually in play, you finish the hole and post your score to an online leaderboard. A few have made birdie, a few hundred have made par, but most end up with six balls left behind in the African jungle and a souvenir hat. Thanks for trying.

For me, if I'm on the second level at TopGolf, I can't follow through to my left side because I'm afraid I'm going to plummet 15 feet onto the artificial grass surface below. So, from a tee box on the edge of a cliff a quarter of a mile above the rocky African outback, I would, more likely than swinging a golf club, be clinging to a rock somewhere well away from the edge.

So, I'll pass. But you have fun.

NOTES

. . . .

. . . .

. . . .

. . . .

❏ **CONQUER THE EXTREME NINETEENTH HOLE** Date: . . . .

CHASE THE MIDNIGHT SUN

Like life itself in the Canadian outback, the golf here is tougher than in our city-adjacent country clubs. How tough? The founders of Yellowknife Golf Club in the Northwest Territories moved the fuselage of a crashed DC-3 to a point near their first tee and called it a clubhouse. That tough. Yellowknife Golf Club wasn't so much designed as it was simply laid down on barren tundra so far north that grass doesn't grow. So, members play from driving range mats on wooden platforms to dirt fairways to artificial turf greens with a local rule that mandates no penalty for players whose ball is stolen by wildlife. That tough.

In the history of the town of Yellowknife, gold and diamonds have been mined but their golf course is anything but a gem. How could it be? There is but a single road leading to Yellowknife, which is so far north it takes 15 hours to drive from Edmonton, which is a six-hour drive north of the Montana border. Yellowknife residents are miners, bush pilots, frontiersmen, and people whose jobs require a John Wayne–like toughness that those of us who sit at a keyboard in an office with an X-Chair can only dream of mustering. But they love their golf and around the time the course opened in 1948 members created the Midnight Classic Golf Tournament to see who really was the toughest.

Up on the sixty-second parallel, where the summer sun on the longest day of the year merely glances off the horizon, they teed off at midnight and played to exhaustion and the last player standing was the winner. Yellowknife legend has it that in the 1970s a gentleman by the name of Sandy Hutchinson played 171 holes in 35 hours before all others cried uncle or surrendered to the black flies. Figuring no one would ever beat that, they turned the event into a more humane tournament, and now they play the Midnight Classic on the weekend closest to the summer solstice with a party and rounds of golf, including one that tees off at midnight but lasts just 18 holes.

NOTES

. . . .

. . . .

. . . .

. . . .

❏ **CHASE THE MIDNIGHT SUN** Date: . . . .

PLAY THE LOWEST AND HIGHEST COURSES

On a Las Vegas vacation I realized I was a day trip from Death Valley, so I gave up on the craps table and rented a car. The only time I had spent below sea level was after being wiped out by a wave in the Atlantic, and so I wanted to see what 282 feet below sea level felt like. I drove to the touristy spots and even without my clubs I visited the Devil's Golf Course, an area of crystalized salt formations deposited by ancient salt lakes and as sharp as coral. There isn't a blade of grass, and the only reason it's called a golf course is thanks to an early guidebook that inexplicitly stated: "Only the devil could play golf on such a surface." I'm not sure even Lucifer would lace up his spikes on such inhospitable terrain.

But just a piece further up Badwater Road you'll find the oasis of Furnace Creek Ranch Golf Course, the lowest real golf course in the world, where it once reached an ambient air temperature of 134 degrees Fahrenheit. The course is 214 feet below sea level and plays to a backdrop of towering craggy and barren mountains, including the 11,049-foot snowcapped Telescope Peak. Furnace Creek is a green oasis in an otherwise monochrome desert landscape. Despite the fact that Death Valley gets less than two inches of rain per year, there are several water holes on the course. And unlike playing at altitude, you'll need to hit more club to cover the distance.

Furnace Creek may not be an oasis like golf-loaded Palm Springs in the desert 250 miles south, but it offers plenty of challenge—including that of the heat, which to get to 134 degrees probably bubbles up from hell.

Getting from Death Valley to Mustang, Nepal, isn't your typical Priceline booking. The flight requires at least two layovers and 24 hours of travel time to get to Kathmandu. Then there's the 18-hour drive to Mustang Golf Course. Make the trip and you'll cover 8,000 miles horizontally and 15,239 feet vertically (pack some Diamox), and if you make the effort, do so for the Top of the World Golf Classic. Few Westerners make the trip, but you might find it worth the trouble. Any player who aces the sixth hole is awarded a horse. Good luck getting that checked through security.

The idea for Mustang Golf Club came from politician Dhara Bista, who extracted one million Nepali rupees from the Constituency Infrastructure Development Fund to build the course. Sounds like one of the great boondoggles of all time, but the expenditure equated to about $7,840. His idea was to promote tourism among bucket list golfers, as if that little thing called Mt. Everest wasn't doing enough for Nepal tourism.

Considering its location, the course is incredibly flat, built on a finger of land amidst some of the most rugged terrain on Earth. But the views are stunning. The air is so thin every swing tires you out, so the tournament is just nine holes. There is other golf in Nepal. The Himalayan Golf Course plays to the magnificent backdrop of the Annapurna mountain range, and Gokarna Forest Golf Resort plays through a small, wooded area just outside the Kathmandu city limits. At less than 5,000 feet above sea level it's up there, but it will be easy breathing for you compared to Mustang.

NOTES

· ·

· ·

· ·

· ·

❑ **PLAY THE LOWEST AND HIGHEST COURSES** Date: · · · · · · · · · · · · · ·

PLAY THE NORTHERNMOST AND SOUTHERNMOST COURSES

I have not yet had the pleasure, but if you find yourself sailing the Northwest Passage, the port of Ulukhaktok on the Canadian island of Victoria offers hunting, fishing, trapping, and the northernmost golf course on Earth. Another 600 miles north of Yellowknife and accessible only by plane or the occasional ship, the term golf course seems a loose interpretation of the nine holes across scrub-covered tundra. Perhaps the only reason for the course being built was because a Scotsman named Billy Joss came to the area to work for the Hudson Bay Company. Like a true Scotsman, Joss brought some clubs and balls with him and on vacant land, which is plentiful near Ulukhaktok, planted nine flags in the tundra and called it golf.

These days the flags are planted in rudimentary artificial green surfaces that appear to be scattered about randomly. Tee boxes are wooden platforms with a small strip of driving range mat to play shots from. There are no fairways, just openness as your target. The artificial greens are hard and next to impossible to land a shot of any length on (and keep it on), so players usually arrive at the green via a bump-and-run attempt.

Old-Time Clubs

Baffy: A golf club of the early days of golf; roughly equivalent to a modern hybrid club.

Cleek: An early metal-head club roughly equivalent to today's driving iron.

Mashie: One of the most commonly used clubs of the nineteenth century, roughly equivalent to a modern 5-iron.

Niblick: Like the mashie, a commonly used club in the nineteenth century. It was a lofted metal-headed club used like today's pitching wedge.

Spoon: A nineteenth-century wooden-head club that is roughly equivalent to today's metal fairway woods.

Every summer the Billy Joss Open Celebrity Golf Tournament raises funds for literacy programs in the northern Canadian outback. It's played over three days and nights under the 24-hour sun. The season is short up here where the record low temperature is -56 degrees Fahrenheit and a July heat wave means the temperature gets into the 60s. In Ulukhaktok you probably won't need those Bermuda-length shorts.

It takes an Aerolíneas Argentinas flight to get you to the so-nicknamed "End of the World"—Ushuaia, Argentina, on the Tierra del Fuego archipelago, where the South American continent is breaking apart little piece by little piece. Here we find the little nine-hole Ushuaia Golf Club, which sits very un-majestically beneath the very majestic southernmost Andean peaks. The snowcapped mountains carry the Martial Glacier almost to the doorstep of Ushuaia, where the nine-hole Ushuaia course with its barely distinguishable fairways and dime-size greens would be a sorry excuse for the only course in a city of about 82,000 if it weren't for the fact that it's just 700 miles from the tip of Antarctica. What this layout lacks in golf standards as recognized by the rest of the world it more than makes up for with the stunning scenery of the snowcapped Chilean Andes. On the longest day of the year (December 21 on this side of the globe) there are more than 17 hours of daylight, and for the visitor it's easy to spend all of them on the course—looking up at the scenery.

NOTES

. . . .

. . . .

. . . .

. . . .

❏ **PLAY THE NORTHERNMOST AND SOUTHERNMOST COURSES**

Date: . . . .

HIT BALLS IN MANHATTAN

Golf can get you to some interesting places and some interesting situations. Like the afternoon I was carrying my bag on the New York City subway system. Sometimes you just look like a goober, and there's nothing you can do about it, and to the largely uninitiated-to-golf New York City subway riders that day, I was the goober.

But my intent was pure and the riders who shared my particular subway car that day might not have understood that I was headed to an oasis of green—albeit artificial—in the hardscape of midtown Manhattan. Chelsea Piers Golf Club offers the next-best thing to golf. You can hit balls toward the Hudson River and the netting will keep you from polluting it. You can take lessons, you can be a member, you can hang out in the clubhouse bar and restaurant. At Chelsea Piers Golf Club you can do everything but actually play golf.

Like the city itself, Chelsea Piers is a melting pot. You find the silky swing of a player who might have been a low-handicapper before taking the Wall Street job. You see the crooked stances and axe-swinging swats of beginners from around the world trying to see what this game is all about. And you work your way through a pre-paid number of balls, each automatically teed up for you. No yellow wire buckets here. In the evening of a crisp spring day the sun sets in the distance over the Hudson, and there's a tranquil feeling that is so infrequent in New York City. And even though you can't record a score and don't move from your designated spot, there's something special about it. Even to a goober like me.

. . . .

. . . .

. . . .

. . . .

❏ **HIT BALLS IN MANHATTAN** Date:. . . . .

PLAY ONE OF THE WORLD'S LONGEST COURSES (FROM THE BACK TEE)

Sometime early in the twenty-first century I found myself standing on the back tee of the first hole of the Pines Course at the International Golf Club in Bolton, Massachusetts, near Boston. At the time it was the longest course in the world, and behind me there was no more room. In front of me lay 8,325 yards of game. I perused the scorecard and wondered how I might negotiate the 715 yards of the par-5 fifth, never mind the two par 5s that played more than 650 yards. I questioned the 567-yard twelfth and how that calculated to be a par 4. I noted the reasonable 180-yard par-3 fourth but then realized it was the diminutive one of the four, the other three playing more than 250 yards each.

My host for the day was a good friend, as were the other two in the foursome, and all were good players, so we accepted the challenge and figured it would make for at least a few good stories for years to come, the best of which was that I shot 76. But I can't really tell the story because I don't remember how I did it. The day was a whirl of well-struck drives that barely reached the fairway, followed by drivers off the deck and full wedges as the third shot on par 4s. I do remember making birdie on a couple of par 5s and taking advantage of the few reasonable-length par 4s.

At some point the Pines Course lost its title as the world's longest course. Now, that belongs to the 8,548-yard Jade Dragon Snow Mountain Golf Club in Lijiang, China. While that may be an impressive scorecard yardage, the course sits at 10,000 feet above sea level, while Bolton sits at 387 feet, where air resistance on a golf ball is much grindier. There are plenty of courses more than 8,000 yards long, but many play at more than 5,000 feet high. The real challenge of length comes closer to sea level at places like the Ross Bridge course on Alabama's Robert Trent Jones Golf Trail, which is 8,191 yards, or, also on the trail, Fighting Joe at Muscle Shoals, measuring 8,092 yards, or the Pete Dye Course at French Lick Resort in Indiana, which plays 8,102 yards.

There is no conversion calculator for altitude and course yardage so who knows how long courses at altitude actually play. I do know that on a warm New England day some summer many years ago, four of us took our blows from then the world's longest course and were satisfied with the outcome. So we went back out and played again.

NOTES

. . . .

. . . .

. . . .

. . . .

❏ **PLAY ONE OF WORLD'S LONGEST COURSES (FROM THE BACK TEE)**

Date:. . . . .

Acknowledgments

This book would not have been possible had my parents, Betty and LeRoy, not left the golf clubs they no longer used while raising six kids in the basement to collect cobwebs and eventually to arouse the curiosity of me and my siblings. To them I am grateful not only for that but so many more important things that shaped who I am. Likewise I am grateful to my kids, Emily, Bridget, and Alex, who allowed me to introduce them to the game and who are still regular playing partners. And to their mother, Reba, who tolerated and occasionally joined those after-school outings at the club. To the hundreds, perhaps thousands, of playing partners I have encountered over the years, many of whom became good friends and all of whom have contributed to my enjoyment of the game, in some way, you are all represented in this book. I hope I have done you all justice.

About the Author

Jeff Thoreson is a golf and travel writer based in Frederick, Maryland. He has written for numerous newspapers and magazines during his 40-year career. He was the founding editor of the *Washington Golf Monthly* and the *GolfStyles* network of regional magazines and edited those publications for more than 25 years. He holds a degree in journalism from the University of Maryland.

His golf journey began by hitting Wiffle balls with his father's clubs in the backyard of his childhood home. He began playing seriously after graduating from college, and progressed from not being able to break 100 without a few mulligans and lengthy gimmies to eventually trying to qualify for the US Amateur. He has played in one professional tournament with a crash-and-burn result. He still travels to play the world's great courses but finds particular pleasure in stumbling across lesser-known gems in faraway lands. He still plays to a 4 handicap.